THE DARK SIDE OF
LIBERALISM

Unchaining The Truth

THE DARK SIDE OF
LIBERALISM
UNCHAINING THE TRUTH

PHIL KENT
PRESIDENT, SOUTHEASTERN LEGAL FOUNDATION

AUGUSTA, GEORGIA

Copyright 2003 by Phil Kent

Library of Congress Cataloging-in-Publication Data
Kent, Phil, 1951-
The dark side of liberalism : unchaining the truth / by Phil Kent.
p. cm.
Includes index.
ISBN 1-891799-09-6
1. Liberalism–United States. 2. United States–Politics and government–2001- I. Title.
JC574.2.U6K45 2003
320.51'3'0973–dc21

                        2003005884

Published in the United States by:
HARBOR HOUSE
629 STEVEN'S CROSSING
MARTINEZ, GEORGIA 30907

Visit us at www.harborhousebooks.com

Distributed to the trade by
National Book Network
15200 NBN Way
Blue Ridge Summit, PA 17214

Printed on acid-free paper
Manufactured in the United States of America
10 9 8 7 6 5 4 3 2 1

Jacket and Book Design by Fredna Lynn Forbes
Author Photography by King and Spivey Artography, Dunwoody, Georgia

Books are available in quantity for promotional or premium use. Write to Director of Special Sales, 629 Stevens Crossing, Martinez, GA 30907, for information on discounts and terms call (706)738-0354.

To my wife Bonnie

TABLE OF
CONTENTS

ACKNOWLEDGEMENTS

*My first book would not have been written without the
sustained encouragement, trust and wisdom of Harbor House
publisher/editor/author Randall Floyd. I also benefited immensely from
the research, editing assistance and advice of my friend Todd Young,
president of an Atlanta public relations/consulting firm. And much
appreciation and love go to my great wife Bonnie and wonderful son
Philip Jr., my main cheerleaders (and critics) throughout this project.*

*For the work she spent coordinating with Randall Floyd editing
my manuscript before it went to press, special thanks goes to veteran
Augusta, Ga., magazine editor Sherry Foster.*

*Friends and colleagues who helped me on specific chapters or
provided ideas include Atlanta writer/researcher Susan Lacetti Myers,
author and Atlanta television personality Dick Williams,
Atlanta Judge Craig Schwall, radio talk show host Austin Rhodes,
researcher S. Angelic Moore, Georgia State University constitutional
law professor L. Lynn Hogue, Southeastern Legal Foundation general
counsel Valle Dutcher Ashley, SLF Development Director Eric Dial
and Augusta, Ga., attorney Mike Carlson.*

*I especially want to thank Georgia businessman Bijon Meemar
for his steadfast support for The Dark Side of Liberalism and
my work at Southeastern Legal Foundation. I also dedicate this book
to the memory of his late brother Kam Meemar, a salt of the earth guy
who was a great American.*

PREFACE

*It's Good To Know Phil Kent's
In The Trenches...*

Conservatives *can* win!

This simple belief, shared by the front-line activists and professionals who man the barricades in America's conservative policy centers and editorial pages, inspired the genesis of this book. The theme, to borrow from fellow activist M. Stanton Evans, is freedom.

In a recent news article in *The Economist* highlighting the triumphs of the so-called conservative "think tanks," the writer points to the fact that many of the most profound social changes caused by government action in the past several decades have been inspired by professional center-right activists. The article describes the think tank world as a de facto "shadow government," reflected in the high number of former think-tankers in the current Bush administration.

The relatively small band of brothers (and sisters) who make up the conservative vanguard of various state and national organizations – as well as the brave few in newsrooms and editorial offices across America – share a fierce commitment to common-sense principles of free enterprise, individual liberty, and the wisdom and relevance of the U.S.

Constitution. These few, speaking clearly and forcefully on behalf of the millions of Americans once described by Richard Nixon as "the silent majority," make up what now-U.S. Senator Hillary Clinton once described in disgust as "the vast right-wing conspiracy."

Described instead by Phil Kent, the author of this book, as the "conspiracy of freedom," the conservative movement has rolled back or kept at bay the most obnoxious threats to liberty and individual self-determination propagated by the left-institutionalized welfare, discriminatory racial and gender quotas, regulatory attacks on the fundamental right to own and enjoy private property, and the pernicious move to squelch the speech of those who voice opinions based on religious faith. Why? Because conservatives believe that the U.S. Constitution means what it says.

But the struggle defined by Pat Buchanan as a "cultural war" is far from victorious. The torrent of left-wing propaganda, fostered by a highly organized, well-funded elite of certain corporate "charitable" foundations, liberal think tanks, and media outlets, more often than not creates the impression in the minds of the silent majority that "there's nothing we can do to stop it."

Consider the facts. Center-right policy centers and public interest law firms receive one dollar of charitable support for every three-and-a-half dollars received by left-wing groups. Until recently, left-leaning groups and politicians received *ten times* the print and electronic news coverage received by conservatives. Until 1994, the Democrats controlled the U.S. House of Representatives for 40 years, and controlled the U.S. Senate for most of that period. Roughly 70 percent of the federal judiciary, at least until 1988, has been populated by center-left judges.

Into this maelstrom ride the conservative "think tankers," led by individuals like Phil Kent, president of Southeastern Legal Foundation (SLF) and former journalist and editorial page editor. As SLF's communications and policy director since 1994, I was thrilled when my friend asked me to assist with *The Dark Side.* For years, I've collected hundreds of requests from SLF supporters across America who visit our web site, receive our mail, call in to our talk radio appearances, and see us on TV and ask, "Can you give us a guidebook for conservatives?"

So began the process of "unchaining the truth."

Who better to write this book, when approached by Harbor House publisher E. Randall Floyd in the late summer of 2002, than Phil, a 25-year, award-winning conservative journalist who leads one of the nation's most effective conservative legal organizations?

With a flood of conservative commentators-cum-authors racing up the bestseller lists, our concerted aim was to draft a working document for conservatives, a "report from the front lines" of today's raging legal and policy battles. This has been accomplished with *The Dark Side* – a behind-the-scenes user's guide for conservatives who want to fight back and win.

I first met Phil in 1995 when, as a recent law school graduate serving as SLF's communications director, I was instructed to "make sure *The Augusta Chronicle's* editorial page editor knows we're going after Bill Clinton's Justice Department." Phil's reputation as a no-nonsense conservative unafraid of ruffling Democrat and liberal feathers across Georgia and the nation made him a unique media resource for SLF's work. He had successfully taken on corrupt government officials at all levels, bringing the light of public scrutiny to the dark corners of many well-entrenched political deals. He had also been sued – unsuccessfully – for doing so.

During our first phone call, Phil greeted me with the standard conservative line, "It's good to know you're in the trenches. I'll do what I can, and keep me informed." As SLF successfully defended retired FBI agent Gary Aldrich's right to publish his explosive bestseller, *Unlimited Access: An FBI Agent Inside the Clinton White House,* against FBI efforts to silence him, Phil predicted that the episode would shake the Clinton mystique to its core. It did.

In the following years, Phil closely tracked SLF's work, successfully defending the integrity of the Census against the Clinton plan to statistically manipulate it for political gain. Again, Phil predicted a U.S. Supreme Court win – and it happened. SLF launched a seven-state crusade to slash the multi-billion dollar "stealth" unemployment insurance taxes paid by employers, and Phil promoted the effort from his editorial office in Augusta, Georgia, poised strategically on the Georgia-South Carolina border. As a result, both states slashed their taxes, as they did when Phil began writing a series of editorials condemning the so-called "intangibles" tax on out-of-state stocks and bonds levied in Georgia.

The U.S. Supreme Court eventually agreed that the taxes were unconstitutional.

And when SLF continued its civil rights litigation challenging illegal government-sponsored race quota programs for public contracting, Phil welcomed the company. More than a dozen years before the U.S. Supreme Court slammed the door on municipal quota programs in its landmark decision *Croson v. City of Richmond* (1989) – a case in which SLF participated as a friend of the court – Phil began calling on local governments to realize the hypocrisy of reverse discrimination. SLF has successfully knocked out unfair quota programs in Richmond, Atlanta, Nashville, and Jacksonville, Florida – and Phil predicted these victories.

So, when the SLF's presidency became available, Phil Kent was a logical choice to head the vigorous organization. Comfortable on national TV, radio talk shows, and with print media, Phil has continued SLF's 27-year David-and-Goliath history of "front-line" assaults on the enemies of liberty. In fact, Phil insists that SLF and other conservative "think tanks" instead be called "*do* tanks." Clearly, with a "conservative's conservative" at the helm of SLF, a book was in order.

As a young man in upstate New York, Phil read former U.S. Sen. Barry Goldwater's *Conscience of a Conservative* and Sen. Strom Thurmond's *The Faith We Have Not Kept*, confirming his lifelong "conservative first" approach to public policy and inspiring him to join the Young Americans for Freedom. After graduating from the Henry W. Grady

School of Journalism at the University of Georgia – during which he led multiple counter-demonstrations to visits by Jane Fonda and other radicals opposing American action in Vietnam – Phil served his country as an Army officer and was honorably discharged as a first lieutenant.

In the early 1980s, Phil did a tour of duty as press secretary for Thurmond, the venerable former Democrat-turned-Republican who helped usher in the so-called "Solid South" conservative voting trends. Marked by consistency of purpose and effort, it must be said that Phil's professional life is a testament to conservative activism.

The Dark Side is itself a testament, carefully crafted as a useful guide for conservatives who, knowing in our hearts we are right, nevertheless seek insight into *how we should fight to win*. As Phil has said, and it bears repeating here for readers seeking successful ways to defend American liberty, "it's good to know you're in the trenches . . . I'll do what I can."

Never give up; conservatives *can* win!

Todd G. Young
President, DecisionMakers
Atlanta, Georgia
March 2003

INTRODUCTION

Why We Believe...Why We Fight

When William F. Buckley Jr. wrote *Up From Liberalism* in 1959, his purpose was to expose "the folklore of American liberalism." In retrospect, knowing what we know now, the liberalism of the 1950s was still just a benign cancer.

As the 21st century unfolds, the past five decades underscore that the political and cultural Left exerted an intolerant and stifling influence that led to an incredible reshaping of American institutions. A dedicated minority can get a lot accomplished, as proven by liberal activists in the universities and the media aided by their truckling judges and politicians. They have reshaped our political discourse, public policies and, indeed, our entire nation for the worse.

The "noble" Franklin Roosevelt-style big government/tax-and-spend liberalism of the 1950s was bad enough. But modern liberalism took on an additional and culturally corrosive aspect in the late 1960s.

The "Woodstock Music and Art Fair's Aquarian Exposition" was held in upstate New York in August 1969. Some still think of it as a time when innocent "flower children" cavorted to the sound of rock music. But Woodstock was far than that. The dawning of the so-called Age of Aquarius came to symbolize the "if it feels good, do it" philosophy of sex and drugs. Never before had state and federal authorities condoned the open and massive use of illegal narcotics in public.

The drug exodus from reality would never have been possible without plenty of help from the Liberal Establishment of the 1960s. Hollywood and the media glorified Woodstock's half-a-million comatose hippies registering "alienation" from their parents, the Vietnam war or whatever else the liberal pundits and professors of the day told them they were "alienated" from.

The Potemkin village of political and cultural liberalism – the great façade where everybody was supposed to be equal, progressive and for peace – was revealed to be a fraud. The Dark Side of Liberalism emerged all too quickly. And the beat goes on.

Woodstock, in turn, fueled the "generation gap" and the "women's liberation" movement of the 1970s. One heard a number of explanations for the "gap," ranging from just plain adolescent rebellion to youthful disgust at adult "materialism." There was some truth in this, but this really didn't explain how the United States became so polarized during the presidency of Richard Nixon. The full unvarnished truth is that it was manufactured and fanned by the Left and its media allies for their dark political purposes.

The great Christian writer C.S. Lewis, back in 1940, envisioned the Devil as declaring in *The Screwtape Letters*:

"And since we cannot deceive the human race all the time, it is very important to us to cut every generation off from all others; for where learning makes a free commerce between the ages there is always the danger that the characteristic errors of one may be corrected by the characteristic truths of another."

A national mood in the 1970s was created – and militantly fostered by the campus Left. Yes, there was the aftermath of the 1960s civil rights battles which the segregationist South was destined to lose. Conservatives still argued for states' rights and the 10th Amendment, but their cause was hurt by the George Wallaces of the day. Conservatives and intellectually honest liberals supported civil rights in the name of equal opportunity. But the 1970s saw the rise of a "black power"/black separatist movement that went way beyond what Martin Luther King Jr. championed.

Furthermore, there was the so-called women's liberation movement.

Constitutional conservatives long argued that every American is equal under the law, and women deserved equal pay for equal work. But, for a time in that decade of turmoil, ideas were no longer accepted because they were true, or rejected because they were false. They were hailed because they were "progressive," or "in." They were junked because they were somehow "fascist" or "out."

The late novelist Taylor Caldwell effectively mocked the "equality" sought by the libbers of the 1960s and the radical Martha Burks of today. "I hope that no man will extend mercy to them because of obvious pregnancies, but will rudely tell them that it is no excuse to shirk a day's heavy labor, and they should be like Russian women. I hope they will be proud when some court demands that they support 'delicate' husbands for a lifetime, and pay alimony. I hope, when they look in their mirrors, that they will be pleased to see bitter and exhausted faces, and that they will be consoled by their paychecks."

She thought women shouldn't be lowered to equality!

And, Caldwell additionally warned, "the strongest sign of the decay of a nation is the feminization of men and the masculinization of women."

It took the winds of the 1980s to blow away some of Woodstock's fallout. Grassroots activist Phyllis Schlafly rallied women around the country to defeat ratification of the phony Equal Rights Amendment to the Constitution – the biggest and most humiliating defeat for liberals since they lost the right-to-work battle in Congress in the mid-1960s.

The election of Ronald Reagan in 1980 broke the 40-year political stranglehold of the Liberal Establishment in Washington. Hollywood finally was forced to split on the drug issue, with some prominent celebrities agreeing with Nancy Reagan to "just say no to drugs." And the AIDs and rising sexual disease rate, especially among minorities and homosexuals, made the unrestrained barnyard sex of Woodstock less appealing.

By 1990 liberals needed a cutting-edge issue to sway opinion to their side again, and another glimpse at their dark side was seen when they injected "multiculturalism" into the nation's political discourse. The balkanization of the country that it fosters attacks the traditional concept of Americanism just as effectively as a bullet fired into the brain. It is now to hell with the national motto *E Pluribus Unum*— "Out of Many, One."

"Diversity" became a new liberal mantra, and many corporate conservatives were even forced to embrace it in the workplace to insulate themselves from charges of "racism." Left-wing activist Jesse Jackson promoted hyphenated Americanism by popularizing the term "African-American." Jackson even led protestors at Stanford University in chanting "Hey, hey, ho, ho, Western Civilization's got to go!"

He had prematurely let the cat out the bag— that slogan is now the main mission of modern, warped liberalism.

At the same time, the uncontrolled legal and illegal immigration of he 1970s and 1980s was working to help liberals "defend the underdog" in the media while helping them gain a political upper hand by forging a potent liberal/minority coalition in some parts of the country, most notably California. If millions of immigrants whose salary is less then $10,000 a year and possess less then an eighth grade education were quickly made citizens and voters, farsighted liberals knew they would be susceptible to every bit of leftist demagoguery imaginable. They know that the traditional Judeo-Christian ethic upon which the country was founded would finally be dynamited, since many of these immigrants shun speaking English and other forms of assimilation into the majority culture.

And, of course, liberals shamelessly push political correctness to exercise mind control over the culture. Free speech, valued by most liberals of the 1950s, is being assaulted not by the Right but by many leading lights of the Left. Restrictive "speech codes" have to be battled at universities.

Furthermore, the benign-sounding Bipartisan Campaign Finance Reform Act was passed by Congress and signed into law in 2002. It severely undercut the right of association and First Amendment speech rights -- particularly, advocacy groups using radio and TV to support or oppose a federal candidate during a primary or general election campaign.

So, just as the Dark Side had to be effectively fought in the Reagan era, it is now time again for a full frontal assault on an even more energized Left that -- with a few notable exceptions like when Newt Gingrich finally forced Bill Clinton to sign sweeping welfare reform-- has been winning far too many victories.

In every challenge, there is opportunity. That's why *The Dark Side of Liberalism: Unchaining the Truth* was written.

Liberals don't have to win every battle by default. Conservatives – characterized by shrill liberals as dull-witted or narrow-minded bigots – nevertheless have opportunities to speak out with forceful clarity to shape the national debate and influence public policies. The good news is that the expansion of Internet use, conservatives' continued domination of talk radio and the expanded opportunities offered by cable television all work in our favor to expose the myths and lies of the opposition.

Each chapter in this book is devoted to a specific topic, beginning with a discussion of the subject and its current status. Following each discussion is either some good news "from the front lines" about the issue or action steps – how conservatives are advancing, or can advance, its cause on the issue.

This book, while chronicling liberalism's Long March and its alarming inroads, seeks to show how to "unchain the truth." It emphasizes how conservatives and their natural allies in Middle America can yell "Stop!" as William F. Buckley labored to do in the 1950s, and be effective in the new century.

Hard-core liberals will never change, but if the counter-argument to them is persuasive enough and can reach enough people, the vast center of the American body politic will side with us. I truly believe that the future of the American republic depends on the conservative, Constitutionalist counter-argument ultimately winning.

CHAPTER ONE

THE RACE DIVIDE:
TODAY'S BATTLES
&
TOMORROW'S VICTORIES

THE LIBERAL LINE

Everybody's equal, but oppressed minorities deserve special preferences. The U.S. is a racist society. Therefore, the criminal justice system is racist, IQ and college admissions tests are racist and, unless regulated by government, businesses are racist. Conservatives are inherently racist, and any non-white conservative is a traitor to his or her race. African-Americans harmed by slavery should be given reparations.

UNCHAINING THE TRUTH

Race relations in the United States experienced shameful lows and exhilarating highs from the time of the painful Southern Reconstruction until the civil rights revolution of the 1960s, which culminated in the passage of the 1964 Civil Rights Acts and the 1965 Voting Rights Act.

But in the pivotal year of 1965, modern liberalism stood at a crossroads.

The movement's leading lights were torn with regard to which road to travel. Was it the vision of equality that, as Martin Luther King said, people should be judged on their character and not on their skin color? Was it the vision U.S. Sen. Hubert Humphrey stipulated, that nothing in the Civil Rights Act (which he helped write) should be construed as giving preference to anyone? Or would skin color become *the* obsession?

The Dark Side obsessed with skin color won that internal debate.

"Whitey" was soon to be demonized— especially by self-hating white liberals.

In 1969, author Susan Sontag was explicit, writing that whites are "the cancer of history." That same year black author James Baldwin, acclaimed by the Dark Side's leading organ, *The New York Times*, proclaimed America to be a Nazi "Fourth Reich."

By the 1990s, the propaganda line was honed so it could become strikingly simple and repetitive, even if it didn't catch on at first: Christopher Columbus and the

European settlers who followed him practiced "genocide" against Indians, and the new nation that became the United States was founded by what most liberal academics now continually disparage as "dead, white males."

Back in the mid-1960s, we were all Americans, even though everybody took pride in their ethnic and cultural background. But a decade later, in a well-executed pincer movement on Middle America executed from "above" and "below," hyphenated-Americans and "victim groups" emerged. The pressure "above" came from left-wing judges, academics and their Big Media allies; it came from "below" via rabble-rousing media darlings like Cesar Chavez and Jesse Jackson, who introduced and popularized the term "African-American."

The concept of the hyphenated American meshed nicely in the 1990s with the introduction of "multicultural-ism" in institutions ranging from schools to corporations. Multiculturalism teaches that all cultures are equal except for the traditional Eurocentric culture upon which the United States was founded. Whites, the liberal party line goes, lack the moral status of a victim group. Therefore, when whites are verbally or even physically attacked, some in the media and judiciary view it as justifiable retribution.

Another fatality of the "debate" over race is free speech. Those who defend themselves from these assaults by citing crime statistics, facts, trends in our culture or even opinions are mugged yet again for using "offensive" or "hate" speech toward minorities.

And talk about a mugging. I attended the 100th

birthday party for then-Sen. Strom Thurmond, R-S.C., where Sen. Trent Lott, R-Miss., attempted to make a light-hearted, innocent – though ill-advised – tribute to the South Carolinian's failed 1948 presidential campaign. I was standing right next to a phalanx of journalists – and they didn't take umbrage. There was no "gasp in the room" after the 1948 campaign remark – although some journalists invented this "news" days later.

Even an intellectually honest liberal who was at the event – former Sen. Paul Simon, D-Ill. – said he saw no bigotry in Lott's remarks. Yet, within a few days, left-wing scribes – and Lott's vocal enemies inside the Republican Party and within the White House – sought to make him crawl through broken glass to apologize for nostalgia regarding racial segregation.

(Lott fumbled his belated responses; he should have quickly and flatly declared that no one could seriously imagine he was for segregation or pined for those days.)

Still, as those few voices who rose to Lott's defense at the time underscored, the Mississippi senator was being accused of a "thought crime." As the days after the party turned into weeks, Lott was asked to apologize for "being for segregation" – a statement he had never made.

But while conservatives can be crucified for "thought crimes," liberal politicians and pundits tend to exonerate remarks of minority members by "understanding" their motives. As this continually occurs, radical members of minorities have little restraint when it comes to utilizing violence.

(There's also growing "jury nullification," whereby minorities on juries refuse to convict fellow minority members.)

Reflect on the Big Media treatment of the innocent white truck driver who was dragged out of his rig and nearly beaten to death by a black mob during the 1991 Los Angeles riot. Compare that TV tape to the familiar film clip of white policemen beating black criminal Rodney King. Which one was aired far more?

Fast forward to late 2002 and recall the Wichita trial of two black brothers later convicted of torturing, raping and killing four young whites. It was an animalistic hate crime surely on a par with the dragging death of James Byrd, a black man, in Texas. Yet liberal editors played to the Dark Side. Virtually no national coverage of the Wichita Horror occurred (with the laudable exception of Fox News Channel).

Indeed, as an editor for years at a medium-size daily newspaper, I saw colleagues at my own paper and others – some of them friends – all too often employing a double standard in race-related coverage (especially playing down or ignoring the foibles or inflammatory statements of powerful minority politicians).

Consider what happened with *The Philadelphia Daily News*. In the interests of its readers and public safety, it published an Aug. 22, 2002, news story with statistics revealing that one in 20 alleged Philadelphia murderers was non-white. The paper even ran front page mug shots of 15 of 41 murder suspects for whom police had outstanding warrants

– and they happened to be black, Hispanic and Asian.

Of course, radicals in the minority community went berserk, and demanded that the editors either be fired or grovel. The liberal trucklers went right along. Guess what happened? The editors apologized! One wrote: "I think the cover was literally correct, but a mistake on our part because what we have to worry about is perceptions, and not just the literal truth."

Hiawatha Bray, an independent Pennsylvania black journalist, fired off the best response to this craven apology.

"A newspaper is apologizing for printing the truth. It's embarrassing and humiliating that so many murders are committed by black people, but it's the job of newspapers to publish embarrassing and humiliating truths. No newspaper editor has any business apologizing for writing truthfully about an issue of obvious pubic concern just because it upset some members of the public. Get a grip, you guys."

Another graphic example of prominent liberals publicly apologizing or excusing away violence was provided after Sept 11, 2001, by Yale University scholar Donald Kagan. He wrote in *Intercollegiate Review* that among the faculties of the prestige universities, the main response to the Muslim terrorist attacks was to sympathize with the angry and bereaved hijackers who, understandably, hated the decadent U.S. culture (apparently epitomized by everything from Coca Cola ads to sexy singer Britney Spears).

Thus, the Dark Side has emerged in recent years: All of these demands and excuses are based upon division, vindictiveness and a desire by "victims" to get even. Those who are "responsible" for causing the "justified" attacks (i.e., white Americans, Jews, or whichever group is labeled as "exploiter") cannot, by the Dark Side's definition, be "victims" themselves, no matter how egregious the attack against them.

Ward Connerly, the courageous black California university system regent, gives an interesting insight on today's race problems based on a fascinating Dec. 19, 1997, White House meeting with then-President Bill Clinton and his vice president. Connerly was joined by U.S. Rep. Charles Canady, R-Fla., scholars Stephan and Abigail Thernstrom and former Labor Secretary Lynn Martin.

The meeting came about because Clinton had earlier launched a national "dialogue on race" which quickly became a monotonous liberal sermon fanned by his official all-liberal race panel headed by historian John Hope Franklin. And since it was obvious that the race cards Clinton 's panel were dealing came from a stacked deck, Clinton did what he did best: arrange a "photo op" meeting with "the opposition" so he could appear open-minded and caring.

But the meeting revealed far more than Clinton wanted revealed. It is important for intelligent Americans to consider what was discussed that afternoon— it is the only honest debate on race that has occurred in the nation since the congressional debates of the mid-1960s. The full blow-by-blow account can be read in Connerly's book, *Creating Equal: My Fight Against Race Preferences* (Encounter Books, 2000).

But several exchanges are highly instructive.

Connerly forthrightly replied to Clinton's introductory hope that we could "move this nation forward" by saying that wouldn't happen "unless we deal with the perception that there are preferences being given to people simply because they check a box and that benefits are conferred on the basis of checking that box."

But it was Al Gore's knee-jerk mindset that really must give pause. Here's how Connerly tells it:

"While the president seemed to be enjoying himself, Vice President Gore had sat stiff as his stereotype, his mouth compressed into a disapproving slit and his eyes boring holes into those of us whose ideas he found distasteful. After remaining silent during the first part of the meeting, he finally spoke up, posing a loaded question to Congressman Canady about whether a community that was half black but with an all-white police force wasn't in clear need of affirmative action in hiring.

"Canady answered that hiring policemen of a certain race to appeal to the racial sensibilities of a part of the citizenry reminded him of the South during Jim Crow. Stephan Thernstrom added that the community he lived in outside Boston was almost all white. Did this mean that the city government should tell qualified blacks applying for the police force to 'go back to Roxbury' and police their own? To Gore's assertion that affirmative action should be credited for much of the progress in integrating big city police forces, Lynn Martin countered that it was actually the end of formal and informal policies of discrimination in the

1960s that had accomplished this."

Of course, because of the forced busing and all those destructive race and gender quotas that Al Gore loves, there is bound to be reaction. We are seeing it already, though belatedly. Americans of good will of all races should consider the following positive developments in the war to maintain the rule of law while re-asserting reason and fairness in the great racial debates of the 21st century.

★ *Race and gender quotas.* The great untold victory for those who believe that everyone ought to be truly treated equally comes in the area of race and gender quotas in public contracting. Since the landmark 1989 U.S. Supreme Court decision, *Croson v. City of Richmond*, not one government-sponsored race-preference quota program for contracting has survived a court challenge. Why? As my organization, Southeastern Legal Foundation, has discovered in challenging race-quota programs, courts continue to find two important legal principles. First, government-sponsored segregation was wrong 40 years ago, and it's just as wrong today when governments discriminate on the basis of race or gender. It's part of the constitutional guarantee of due process and equal protection, affirmed by the 1964 Civil Rights Act. Second, the only legal quota based on race or gender can come from proof that the program is remedying specific wrongs done by a government today.

★ *Legal affirmative action.* Legal affirmative action programs, which focus on non-protected legal classifications such as economic need, can be and are being developed in many cities across the nation. In 1993, when Detroit's race quota program for public contracting was struck down as unconstitutional by a federal court, Mayor Dennis Archer instituted a color-blind program for contracting. The program focuses on city-owned businesses and objectively defined "disadvantaged" businesses. Today, the program has a higher minority participation rate than the old, illegal quota program.

★ *Multicultural juries rejected.* The multiculturalism celebrated by the Left is finally being battled in the justice system. In early 2002, the Second Circuit U.S. Court of Appeals erected, in the words of legal analyst Bruce Fein, "a laudable wall" in *U.S. v. Lemrick Nelson and Charles Price.* The federal prosecutions of Nelson and Price had its genesis in Brooklyn, N. Y., after a Jewish driver struck two black children, leaving one dead and the other injured. Blacks gathered at the accident scene, and voiced outrage over the appearance of a Jewish hospital ambulance to assist the Jewish driver before city ambulances could treat the children. It was then that Price yelled at the crowd saying, among other things, "We can't take this anymore. They're killing our children. The Jews get everything they want. The police are protecting them." Then he exhorted the crowd: "Let's get the Jews. An eye for an eye." Of course, the crowd turned violent, torching cars and assaulting Jews. Nelson was arrested for stabbing a Jewish rabbinical student to death. The federal judge presiding over the case feared a Los Angeles-style riot if guilty verdicts occurred. So Judge David Trager manipulated the rules, contrary to federal criminal procedure, to ensure there would be three blacks, one professed Jew and one with Jewish parents. Guilty verdicts were nevertheless returned against both defendants, and both challenged the jury selection. Writing for a three-judge Second Circuit appellate panel, Judge Guido Calabresi criticized racial or religious quotas in jury selection as unconstitutional stereotyping. As Fein asked in an analysis of the case: "There's no exception to mollify private community prejudices or enmities. Where would be the stopping point? Would Jewish Defense League members accused of crimes against Muslims be entitled to a 50 percent Jewish jury?"

★ *Radicals rejected.* While political redistricting by state legislatures can create "safe" non-competitive districts for Democrats or Republicans, there are indeed ways to defeat an entrenched incumbent when there is an opponent of note. A textbook case is the 2002 primary defeat of U.S. Rep. Cynthia McKinney, D-Ga. The most anti-white, America-bashing member of Congress had been protected and pampered by Georgia's Democrat-dominated legislature – yet no one could ultimately protect McKinney from the thousands of voters in her district who normally voted Republican but crossed over into the Democratic primary to vote for her centrist black opponent. Also contributing to her defeat were pockets of black middle- to upper class voters tired of her embarrassing outbursts. Particularly fascinating is that the GOP crossover vote was coordinated over the Internet. It only took a few grassroots activists to create a website that got close to a million hits leading up to the primary. Its phone call lists were distributed as spreadsheets in e-mail attachments. In fact, organizers raised most of their money through credit card contributions made over the Internet from all over the United States. It was a district no Republican could ever win, but clever center-right grassroots opposition made sure that the nation's No. 1 black racist was defeated.

★ *Racial profiling.* When John Ashcroft became attorney general, he tried to placate critics by meeting with the Congressional Black Caucus and announcing that ending "racial profiling" was his top priority. When Sept. 11 occurred, he no doubt wished he hadn't thrown them this needless sop. The Justice Department immediately detained 75 immigrants —.001 percent of the Arab population of the U.S. – yet the Left and its domestic Muslim chorus went ballistic. "War on Terrorism Stirs Memory of (Japanese) Internment" was the screaming Sept. 24 *New York Times* headline. Then Ashcroft's department interviewed 5,000 young Muslim males. The criticism intensified, even though police traditionally canvas "the usual suspects" and use a dragnet after a serious crime – and the Sept. 11 attack was a serious crime inflicted on innocents. The Dark Side was again exposed to the light of day during Senate Judiciary Committee testimony that "fears of racial profiling did impede the FBI's terrorism investigation of Arab men" at flight training schools. FBI Director Robert Mueller continued with a carefully-worded but amazing admission: "I've seen indications of concerns about taking certain action, because that action may be perceived as profiling." Has the word "profiling" become demonized by the Left? Maybe, maybe not. Yet this author travels frequently, and ever since the Sept. 11 attacks I've queried dozens and dozens of airline passengers regardless of race or gender about passenger screening. All respondents flatly say particular scrutiny must be given to Middle Eastern men. (If leading spokesmen for America's Muslim community had quickly reinforced this message, it would have been better for all concerned.) The Computer-Assisted Passenger Profiling System utilized by airports analyzes patterns such as cash payments for tickets and one-way trips. It simply needs to include national origin and gender! The large majority of Americans, as the war on terrorism continues, will tune out "politically correct" arguments. Also, the glaring failure of police to compile an accurate, early profile of the two black men arrested for the 2002 Washington-area sniper killings – which terrorized hundreds of thousands – further undermines anti-profiling arguments.

★ *The IQ debate.* The Left has never wanted open scientific inquiry into how IQ relates to race, so the past 30 years have seen researchers ranging from Arthur Jensen to William Shockley being censored and harassed. (They needn't have worried about Shockley, at least as a lecturer. When I attended a 1974 speech at the University of Georgia – which was ultimately broken up by demonstrators – Shockley's subject matter, replete with indecipherable charts, was completely over students' heads anyway.) *The Bell Curve* by Charles Murray and Richard Hernnstein later broke new ground and gained public attention because the book's critics blasted IQ tests (and student SAT tests) as "culturally biased." That seminal work emboldened other researchers, as evidenced by Dr. Richard Lynn's 2001 book *IQ and the Wealth of Nations,* in which he examined the correlation between a country's wealth and the average IQ of its citizens. The U.S. Supreme Court then waded into the IQ thicket in 2002 by ruling that the Constitution spared a murderer named Daryl Atkins from being electrocuted if he could prove he was "retarded." In other words – as the inimitable Ann Coulter pointed out at the time – "Atkins avoids his capital sentence if he is at least smart enough to know how to fail an IQ test." So the Left plods along ignoring its double standard. It pooh-poohs IQ tests (the Supreme Court once ruled it violates the Civil Rights Act if used in hiring), yet a Supreme Court majority now acknowledges that violent crimes are linked to low IQ!

★ *Reparations for slavery.* White leftists and their noisy minority allies started far too soon with their greedy demand for reparations. In fact, victory over this absurd idea in both the courts of law and the court of public opinion seem well within grasp. It could be the biggest defeat liberalism has suffered since the rejection of the Equal Rights Amendment. Should black people – or groups representing them – be given money for slavery? Of course not. Furthermore, where would the money come from? The failed "Great Society" programs, for which taxpayers paid trillions of dollars, did little to address the underlying causes of minority poverty – failed public schools, dangerous streets, and the rise of the criminal gang. Yet in 2001, the

Internal Revenue Service embarrassingly admitted to "refunding" hundreds of millions of dollars for false claims for "reparations." These demands are more an attack on history and a tool to try to stoke white guilt – not to mention the near-impossible task of proving actual harm to descendants of slaves. And what of the actual descendants of slaveholders? Did not millions of Americans die in a war ostensibly fought to end slavery in the U.S.? Of course, for the record, it was the United States and Britain that led the world in abolishing slavery. The worst slavery occurring today is in Africa, and it involves blacks or Arabs enslaving blacks. Black people, even those descended from slaves, should no more desire the paternalism and favoritism of "reparations" than any other proud race that has had its ups and downs in world history.

❧ UNCHAINED TRUTH ❧
FACTS, TALKING POINTS TO REMEMBER & USE

☆ The struggle for racial equality, best demonstrated by non-violent persuasion resulting in passage of the 1964 Civil Rights Act, was hijacked by radical self-promoters like Jesse Jackson and others. The noble struggle for a level playing field and non-discrimination was turned by radicals into a never-ending effort to promote groups based on skin color at the expense of other groups based on skin color.

✯ The concept of "affirmative action" was originally intended to help level the playing field in America's marketplace made uneven by past discrimination. Laws were put in place to punish those who discriminate based on race.

✯ Too many local, state and federal governments chose the path of further discrimination in the form of racial quotas – for government contracting, schools, college admissions, and employment.

✯ The U.S. Supreme Court has ruled and reaffirmed time and again that governments, with rare, narrow-tailored exceptions, cannot discriminate solely on the basis of race; this is a well-settled area of our law.

✯ The better response to past injustice is to ensure justice today – enforce anti-discrimination laws, improve educational opportunities, and promote legal affirmative action based on need and location, not race and gender.

✯ The term "racial profiling" is a creation of the radical movement to address a more specific concern – fairness in law enforcement. Rather than helping those who may have suffered because of baseless discrimination, the racial profiling cause has instead impeded the ability of legitimate law enforcement efforts.

✯ "Cultural bias" in terms of objective testing continues to be a darling of the radical movement. Made "legitimate" by a minority of individuals with academic credentials, cultural bias hinges on the concept that testing should be designed to "include" various cultural references rather than to focus on objective measures of mathematic and linguistic knowledge.

✭ The Dark Side is whipping up a reparations-for-slavery campaign. Yet many Americans – black and white – died ending America's terrible chapter of black slavery. How can we as a nation put a price on slavery, and on those lives given to end it? And why should Americans whose ancestors never owned slaves nor condoned the practice be punished?

CHAPTER TWO

THE TRUTH
ABOUT IMMIGRATION

THE LIBERAL LINE

Immigration is the cornerstone on which this nation was built. Open borders, especially with our neighbor to the south, gives America the rich "melting pot" that highlights our diversity. Undocumented workers take jobs Americans don't want. A visa lottery bringing in more outsiders, as well as generous refugee resettlement policies, helps enrich America. As for those from other nations now within our borders, it is our duty to provide every social benefit and every protection of the law. English doesn't have to be the common language.

UNCHAINING THE TRUTH

Is the United States of the 21st century an economic giant with clay feet, poised at some point to crash down like a Roman Empire which, in its dying stages, pitifully invited all the barbarians into its gates as "Roman citizens"?

A country like ours that will continue to allow hundreds of thousands of unassimilable illegal aliens to sneak into its borders annually, with strapped taxpayers underwriting them for everything ranging from education to medical services, cannot survive intact over the next few decades. And what a golden opportunity it would then be for this nation's traditional Third World enemies to deliver the *coup de grace!* From a historical point of view, wouldn't they be "just" in using the very same argument to support a continued invasion of the American continent by their undernourished masses as did the European empire builders in the 15th century?

Today's liberals fall into roughly two camps: They either could care less (while celebrating "diversity") or actively seek to change the present United States into, say, a multicultural Third World version of Brazil. When that happens, don't even be surprised to see liberals opting to change the American flag – the beautiful Star - Spangled Banner which so many fought and died for since 1776 – because it is "racist" and "offensive" to foreigners.

Even now the Left's supreme battle-ax, Hillary Clinton, says she wants to change the Pledge of Allegiance to the Flag. But more about that later.

It's up to conservative leaders, opinion-molders and activists to rally the Middle American majority – which still believes that this nation should retain its Western cultural foundation, its common language and especially its rule of law – to severely curb illegal and legal immigration. Conservatives must win this battle over the next 10 years, even if we lose most others (which we won't!)

In the heat of this battle, I predict, conservatives will find a growing number of unusual allies in apolitical or politically disconnected young people who appreciate "green space" and who come to realize that an open border policy means more forests chopped down, more concrete poured for more highways, more pollution and more urban sprawl. Check it out. The Sierra Club is split right down the middle on this issue.

I'm tired of hearing sentiments like "undocumented workers are doing the jobs no other Americans will do." Mark Krikorian of the Center for Immigration Studies, has an excellent response to this cliché:

"If immigration were reduced, and not enough Americans were willing to take those jobs at existing wages, two things would happen: 1) Employers would seek to attract new workers, through higher wages, more benefits and better working conditions, and 2) Employers would seek to eliminate the jobs they were now having trouble filling." That means, essentially, that poor people would get a pay raise! Krikorian logically continues this line of thought:

"Immigration creates more immigration, and the development of industries where immigrants are concentrated is distorted by the huge and continuous supply of cheap foreign labor. In California, for instance, the acreage planted in labor-intensive fruits and vegetables has been steadily increasing, precisely because farmers are basing their planning on the expectation that the illegal flows won't be cut off. If the inflow of illegal workers were reduced, and the outflow were increased, farmers would start making different choices – i.e., planting carrots instead of strawberries, since the harvest of carrots is mechanized."

The Center for Immigration Studies has found unchecked immigration has the effect of slowing technological development in industries that have become addicted to it. Whether it is agriculture, construction or even the restaurant industry, Krikorian notes the incentive to produce more output with fewer workers is diluted because of the loose labor market created by immigration.

The indefatigable Americans for Immigration Control sponsored a highly instructive poll in the summer of 2002 by Zogby International. It asked Americans what they thought about immigration, and the large majority opposed it. Pollsters even asked Mexicans in Mexico about it. Fifty-eight percent of Mexicans surveyed agreed with the statement, "The territory of the United States' Southwest rightly belongs to Mexico." Only 28 percent disagreed, and 14 percent weren't sure. (As columnist Sam Francis wryly notes, "the last category would make good editorial writers for *The Wall Street Journal.*")

No wonder so many Mexicans, with the connivance of their 48 consulates around the U.S., feel free to just unlawfully sneak into our country while bringing their children. It is, as Pat Buchanan points out in his book *Death of the West,* a re-conquest – *La Reconquista.* Mexicans push out Americans, refuse to speak English and simply establish a de facto Mexican province.

The dirt-poor town of El Cenizo, Texas, is a perfect example. Its city commission in August 1999 changed its official language from English to Spanish. (Ordinances can be translated into English, if someone requests it.) Of course, when large pockets of immigrants in other parts of the country feel they don't need to learn the common tongue of English anymore, the U.S. will simply become a Tower of Babel which will only lead to more ethnic division.

Then-Gov. George W. Bush and the Texas attorney general had little to say about El Cenizo. When I interviewed then-presidential candidate Bush in Augusta, Ga., soon afterward and asked about the town's jettisoning of English, he admitted "I don't like it" and offered that his state attorney general "should do something about it." (But nothing happened.)

The future president also playfully exclaimed: "You must be a Pete Wilson Republican" (a reference to California's former governor who supported immigration curbs and opposed bilingualism). I laughed and before having a chance to reply he charmingly continued: "In Texas, I made sure that every high school graduate is required to be proficient in English. Pete Wilson didn't even do that in California." *Touche!*

By the time of Bush's election, surveys were showing

that the vast majority of Americans (including 80 percent of Hispanic immigrants) desired English as the common tongue. And while it received little notice outside of southern California, let's hope the Bush White House reflected on the stunning recall of Hispanic radical and Santa Ana, Ca., School Board President Nativo Lopez on Feb. 4, 2003.

Santa Ana is the most heavily Spanish-speaking city in the U.S. – and it has been dominated in recent years by a cut-throat political machine headed by Lopez. California's Proposition 227 in 1998 limited Spanish-language instruction to one year unless parents received waivers. Well, Lopez tirelessly advocated bilingualism (while once saying he wanted to drive "Anglos" out of the public schools), barely got elected and later convinced a school board majority to let him traipse about the district urging parents to seek waivers. (Almost immediately, situations arose where English-speaking kindergartners were assigned to classrooms in which instruction was entirely in Spanish—and there was no way to opt out.)

For every action there is eventually a reaction, so a disgusted coalition of parents from all backgrounds met to work the streets to secure the required signatures to get a recall of Lopez on the ballot. The incumbent sent up phone banks and eventually spent $150,000 – yet only eked out 3,700 votes in a city with 30,000 identifiable Hispanic voters. Ron Unz, chairman of English for the Children, said "nearly all those Latinos who voted against him cited his support for bilingual education." The Dark Side took a severe hit with Lopez's defeat that day.

What else is to be done? Consider these positive developments:

★ *The Immigration Reform* Caucus in the U.S. House of Representatives was established and is chaired a courageous patriot, Rep. Tom Tancredo, R-Colo. It is a bipartisan group and, especially after the Sept. 11, 2001, attacks, its voice and influence have become stronger. At one point, angry Bush advisor Karl Rove – an advocate for illegal amnesty for millions of illegal aliens – declared Tancredo to be *persona non grata* at the White House. That backfired with most of the House GOP caucus. In fact, Rep. Tom DeLay, R-Tex., and Tancredo engineered a rare defeat for the Bush administration when it refused to ratify the 245(i) amendment which would have legalized some illegal immigrants, including potential terrorists. By the way, is your U.S. representative a member of the Immigration Reform Caucus and, if not, why not?

★ *A non-conservative, Roy Beck,* has emerged as an eloquent spokesman against open borders and his Numbers USA organization has an impressive website. Just like the America First Committee of pre-World War II days included prominent liberals and conservatives so, too, is the immigration reform movement attracting a broader-based coalition. Former Democratic Gov. Dick Lamm of Colorado is also an effective spokesman . Everyone can eat at the table, of course, but conservatives must be in control of the menu.

★ *More segments of the media* are coming around to spotlight the great danger unchecked immigration poses. The Fox TV news operation has done an outstanding job in recent years with news stories and commentary programs forcing public attention on illegal immigration and how the U.S. Immigration and Naturalization Service has been the most dysfunctional agency in the government. (The INS became part of the new Cabinet-level Homeland Security Department in 2003.) More daily newspapers, even if they have liberal editorial pages, are publishing stories, columns and letters ranging from topics like the massive cost of subsidizing illegals to the slippage of English language usage and the failure of "bilingual education" in schools. One pithy quote in a Dec. 26, 2001, letter to the editor of *The Arizona Republic* stands out: "What is the incentive for districts to teach the (non-English-speaking students) English so well that they become reclassified and move entirely to the mainstream? The districts would not only lose money but federal program directors and bilingual teachers would be out of work."

★ *The Sept. 11 assaults* forced President Bush and Congress to focus on implementing a better computer tracking system of foreign students, visa processing reform and the fingerprinting of all visa-holding foreigners coming in or out of the United States. It also thankfully renewed debate on whether U.S. military units, or at least National Guard troops in key states, should augment border security. (A 2002 Zogby poll found 68 percent of Americans wanted the military deployed to help stop illegal immigration.) Whether Congress continues to appropriate adequate money for overall border protection in coming years remains to be seen— so that's why citizen pressure on their members of Congress continues to be imperative.

★ *Pressure on illegal immigrants* working in this country

continues to mount from, of all places, the Social Security Administration. Starting in April 2002, Social Security revved up its program of notifying employers when there is a problem matching employee names with Social Security numbers. In 2002 an estimated 750,000 letters were sent. (Only 110,000 such letters were mailed in 2001.) The no-match letter points out discrepancies and asks employers that they be rectified in 60 days. (Under federal law, any employer who knowingly hires an illegal alien is subject to fines and even prison.) The welcomed result is that many illegal workers are leaving their jobs and going back to their native country. As an elated Nebraska-Iowa district INS director underscores, "This should send a signal that it is not worth the risk to come to this country illegally, pay a smuggler to get you over the border and buy fake documents."

★ *Popular books continue to be written* – and, more importantly, read—on the danger of open borders and the need for large-scale redress. One book in 2002, Michelle Malkin's *Invasion: How America Still Welcomes Terrorists, Criminals and Other Foreign Menaces to Our Shores*, exposes how the process of U.S. immigration policy and its appeals system is flawed. Though herself the daughter of immigrants, she effectively skewers "all the hyphenated groups objecting to every single reasonable immigration measure; those groups do not speak for the majority of immigrants who are here legally."

★ *In my view,* one of the core problems that helped get our nation into this mess – aside from the Kennedy immigration law of 1965 that shifted the immigration entry numbers to favor the Third World – is a continuing misrepresentation and misinterpretation of the Fourteenth Amendment by liberals. They say that the children of illegal aliens born on U.S. soil are to be granted automatic citizenship. But why?

In 1999 then-Rep. Brian Bilbray, R-Ca., first introduced his "Citizenship Reform Act" that would allow only the children of permanent legal residents to be eligible for U.S. citizenship by birth. The issue is not just about money, although this misinterpretation has put a tremendous, multibillion dollar taxpayer strain on our welfare system. It is also about fairness to those who play by the rules, enter this country legally under the most generous legal immigration policy on earth, and wait years to go through the naturalization process to become a permanent resident and then a citizen.

The federal government created this loophole; it is up to Congress to close it. This is an excellent issue for the immigration reform lobby to keep campaigning for – even if it takes another few years of battling the Left to achieve victory. After all, unchecked immigration must now be treated first and foremost as a national security issue.

There is even more insanity. It's a "luck of the draw" visa lottery established by Congress in 1990 – and yet to be repealed – that has admitted hundreds of thousands of additional foreigners whether they are skilled or unskilled, educated or uneducated. Proponents wanted to compensate for a situation in which most visa slots were dominated by people from just a few countries. Well, their wish has come true. My research indicates that among the nationalities benefiting the most in recent years from this congressional gimmick are Bangladesh, Morocco, Egypt and Sudan (once home to Osama bin Laden).

The lottery didn't make any sense at it creation. Now, in an age when homeland security should be paramount, isn't it dangerous to randomly select foreigners from countries the State Department warns are known to support and harbor Islamic terrorists? The FBI worries about al Qaeda sleeper cells in the U.S. There's no question in my mind that they are here in large measure because of the stupid, unmonitored "diversity" visa lottery.

Finally, there's one last bit of mindless do-gooding when it comes to our federal government's overly-generous refugee resettlement policy. The government enters into various agreements with the United Nations on what foreigners will be taken in as officially-designated "persecuted" refugees. One tribe – Somalia's Bantus who are estimated to number approximately 900,000 – has been attacked over the past decade by other Somali clans and many Bantus were resettled by the UN in neighboring Kenya. The African country of Mozambique – the Bantu ancestral homeland – initially agreed to resettle up to 12,000 of them but later backed out. Now, guess what? In early 2003 the U.S. State Department and the federal Office of Refugee Resettlement foolishly agreed to resettle these primitive people in various U.S. cities.

The Bantus don't know any English but, beyond that, don't even understand how automobiles, washing machines or other modern appliances operate. Their problems were graphically summed up by an International Organization for Migration official Shasha Chanoff: "Do not assume they can open a door just because it has a doorknob."

DeKalb County, Georgia, is one of the urban areas where some of the Bantus are to be placed in apartment buildings. An *Atlanta Constitution* reporter found that, even when some of the refugees have been given orientation sessions about how to utilize an apartment (subsidized by the U.S. taxpayer) they still ask: "But where do we build our camp fire?" In fact, law enforcement officials tell me that apartment fires have become commonplace in Atlanta and a dozen other big cities where Third World immigrants unfamiliar with modern ways attempt to cook and then start fires that often destroy entire housing complexes and kill neighbors. Isn't it an incredible disservice to these people for liberal do-gooders to thrust them into totally unfamiliar situations?

Thomas Allen, a one-time refugee worker, notes, "For a fraction of the money the U.S. will spend moving this tribe to America, Mozambique could have been persuaded to carry through on its promises. But the U.S. refugee industry needs clients! So that option was never considered." Clearly, Congress has more work cut out for it: Amend complex refugee laws to 1) safeguard both this nation and poor peoples totally unequipped to live here, and 2) protect the U.S. from questionable asylum seekers who claim "persecution."

☙ Unchained Truth ❧
Facts, Talking Points To Remember & Use

★ The U.S. has the most generous legal immigration policy in the world. The fact that hundreds of thousands sneak into the U.S. each year undermines the rule of law and threatens our national security. Illegal aliens are lawbreakers and should not be rewarded.

★ Don't be fooled by arguments that American industry needs "undocumented" workers. Granted, some legal guest worker programs (agriculture, the hotel and restaurant industry, etc.) are in disarray and need to be reformed. But the only people for whom illegal workers are "good" are unethical employers who exploit them. Illegal aliens are paid slave wages and often live in slave-like circumstances, as evidenced the federal case against Tyson Food Inc. managers charged with smuggling. That is not "good business" because illegal workers do not pay taxes. And the American taxpayer pays billions per year to support illegal aliens with government services, schools, and welfare.

★ After every wave of immigration in U.S. history, there has been a reasonable period for the legal newcomers to assimilate and learn English. Since 1980, there has been no such "cooling off" period – and there have even been amnesties allowing those who snuck in to stay, thus acting as a magnet for future illegal immigration.

⭐ It's not good politics to pander to any ethnic group, no matter what influence they may or may not have. Yet many Democrat and Republican leaders pander to Hispanic groups with proposals to grant yet another amnesty to millions of illegal immigrants in hopes of attracting future voters.

⭐ Open borders are a threat to U.S. national security. Most of the Sept. 11 Muslim terrorists were illegal aliens, possessing "official" documentation like driver's licenses and student visas. Government entities and banks should not empower any undocumented foreigner by recognizing as valid ID the certificates issued by their foreign consulates (particularly the *matricula* IDs issued by Mexico).

⭐ Polls show the large majority of Americans (and 80 percent of legal immigrants) want English retained as our common tongue. If public school English language instruction is discouraged or ended in favor of bilingual or multilingual programs, the common thread that holds this nation together will ultimately be severed.

⭐ It is foolish to allow the child of illegal immigrants born on U.S. soil to automatically become a U.S. citizen. It's equally absurd for Congress to allow continuation of a "diversity" visa lottery that continues to admit foreigners willy-nilly – even from countries on the U.S. terrorist watch list.

⭐ Revise our expensive, overly-generous federal refugee

resettlement policy that often brings in Third World immigrants ill-equipped to function in a modern society.

CHAPTER THREE

AN ISLAMIC WAR
ON THE UNITED STATES

THE LIBERAL LINE

Islam is a peaceful religion, and the United States shouldn't single it out as a threat to national interests - besides, all religions are equal. We should never engage in "profiling" against Muslims in our country. Multiculturalism requires we respect Islam and all its cultural aspects in our own society. The "right wing" is paranoid about an Islamic fifth column.

UNCHAINING THE TRUTH

The twenty-something college co-ed I interviewed in an Atlanta restaurant said she was an Iranian-American brought up as a Muslim. She openly talked of how she shed the dogmatic Islamic radicalism of her father while appreciating freedom, religious tolerance and other attributes of the America she had adopted and come to cherish. I asked, "Is Islam essentially a violent religion?" and she unhesitatingly answered, "Unfortunately, it is."

Dozens of impromptu "on the street" conversations over the past year with individuals raised as Muslims elicited similar answers. Some also explained that American Muslims – who can be patriotic citizens, and many of them are – repeatedly are encouraged from abroad to resort to violence against the United States and the Christian West.

In fact, *Washington Times* editor-at-large Arnaud de Borchgrave reports that Islamists, or radical Muslims, in Pakistan believe that "in the next 10 years, Americans will wake up to the existence of an Islamic army in their midst – an army of jihadis who will force America to abandon imperialism and listen to the voice of Allah."

All too many liberals don't see this. Part of their trendy new religion is "multiculturalism," which requires tolerance of Islam and its attitudes on everything from the rape of women to the barbaric practice of genital mutilation. What's worse is that many liberals (and some misguided conservatives) condemn "profiling" of Muslims when it comes to security checks (such as at airports) and try to explain away any major Islamic threat as overblown hysteria.

It is impossible, though, to ignore the common thread that links all radical Muslims – that Islam is engaged in a great worldwide battle with infidels, the outcome of which will shape the future of the world. Bernard Lewis, in a compelling essay titled "The Revolt of Islam" in the Nov. 19, 2001, *New Yorker*, emphasizes that "it is surely significant that the Koranic and other inscriptions on the Dome of the Rock, one of the earliest Muslim religious structures outside Arabia, built in Jerusalem between 691 and 692 A.D., include a number of directly anti-Christian polemics: 'Praise be to God, who begets no son, and has no partner,' and 'He is God, one, eternal. He does not beget, nor is he begotten, and he has no peer.'"

When the United States in February 2003, announced an elevated "Code Orange" alert, more than one observer began noting that these terror alerts were tying in perfectly with the Muslim religious calendar. After all, it's no secret that U.S. intelligence picks up increased cellular telephone and other "chatter" suggesting that Muslim jihadis hope to link the major Muslim holidays with terrorism against the infidels. At that time, the holiday was Hajj, the pilgrimage to Saudi Arabia that many Muslims make.

Ironically – and *Washington Times* columnist Diana West is to be credited for researching this – the millions of people who traveled to Mecca to hear that Islam is supposedly a peaceful religion instead heard the head Saudi cleric rail to pilgrims that "the enemy has exposed his fangs."

Even the Saudi government announced its intent to

crack down hard on any Hajj-related violence. Yet, at that time, the Council on American-Islamic Relations still had the nerve to label Western and Saudi intelligence connections to terror and Muslim religious holidays as "unnecessary linkage."

The Council has further trouble trying to explain away examples of this worldwide battle as evidenced by growing arrests of Muslim Americans by U.S. law enforcement. In Seattle, James Ujaama is accused by the government of establishing an al Qaeda training camp. In Portland, the U.S. Justice Department found one of six arrested Muslims joined the U.S. Army reserve in order to gain skills to kill Americans. Court affidavits reveal two of six Muslim Americans living near Buffalo, N.Y., possessed audiotapes calling for martyrdom, one of which appealed for "fighting the West and invading Europe and America with Islam."

There is also stark evidence that the prime motivation of the Muslim arrested as the so-called Washington, D.C., sniper was hatred of America. A friend quotes John Allen Muhammad saying that the Sept. 11 terrorist attacks "should have happened a long time ago."

Was he crazy, or a jihadi? Probably both. But taken in context, these examples make clear that hatred of America, the West, and Israel are fast becoming one and the same.

Enaam M. Arnout, the Arab American director of an Islamic charity in this country that federal prosecutors believe funded al Qaeda, finally admitted to funneling money illegally to Muslim fighters in Bosnia and Chechnya in the 1990s. The Arnout case, like the scandal involving the wife of Saudi Arabia's ambassador to the U.S., exposes an unpleasant truth. Almost all members of the Saudi royal family belong to the extremist Wahhabi sect of Islam. The ambassador's wife – a princess – and her husband well know that the Wahhabi clerics regularly preach contempt for Christians, Jews and moderate Muslims. They also know that this same Wahhabi hierarchy operates "charitable" institutions like the Muslim World League, the World Assembly of Muslim Youth and the International Islamic Relief Organization (which have U.S. offices) that have, or are, funding terrorists.

How did the United States come to the point that it is confronted by well-funded and ever-bolder attacks from radical Muslims? Consider two historical developments.

First, there's no question one problem is a pro-Israel foreign policy pursued by most American presidents since 1948 (Dwight Eisenhower, Jimmy Carter and the first President Bush being exceptions). Does Israel – or at least the Jewish state before the 1967 war – have a right to exist? Of course. Every people deserves the right to self-determination, including the Palestinians. There should be a Palestinian state, but our ally Israel fought hard against the concept until some of its visionary leaders changed course in the 1990s.

Unfortunately, terrorist-tainted Palestinian Authority Chairman Yasir Arafat has been the worst possible leader for his dispossessed people. And, for that matter, then-general Ariel Sharon acquiesced to massacres of Palestinians by pro-

Israeli militia in 1982 and, later as Israel's prime minister, to extremely harsh treatment of occupied West Bank and Gaza Arabs.

Since the U.S. hasn't always been an honest broker of the Mideast peace process, our nation and its people are paying the price. This author is not unsympathetic to the general view of former presidential candidate/author Pat Buchanan and his *American Conservative* magazine that the United States shouldn't needlessly pick a fight with Iraq or other Arab states lest we alienate the entire Arab world.

On the other hand, even if Washington's foreign policy and military aid had scrupulously charted an even-handed course toward Arab and Jew, the jihadists and Saddam Hussein-types would still have targeted the "Great Satan" of America one day.

Alexis de Tocqueville, visiting America in 1836, rightly predicted that the rise of technology and statism left two choices for modern man: the free republican form of government he chronicled in America, or the tyranny he saw in Russia and other countries. World history is still a struggle between freedom and tyranny; the war with radical Islam is just the latest manifestation.

So Buchanan and President George Bush surely agree on one important common denominator: Those who are not with us in the war on terrorism are against us. It is the proper strategy to resist the "Religion of Peace" jihadists over the next decade to ensure American interests.

Aside from the Israeli-Palestinian conflict, there is a second, broader answer to the oft-asked post-Sept. 11 question as to "why do they hate us?" Lewis, in his previously cited *New Yorker* piece, notes that America's new role – and the Middle East's perception of it – was illustrated in Pakistan in 1979. Muslim radicals seized the Great Mosque in Mecca and temporarily held it against Saudi police. They proclaimed they were "purifying Islam" and wanted to liberate the holy land of Arabia from the royal "clique of infidels" and the corrupt religious leaders who supported them. As Lewis recorded: "Their leader ... denounced Westerners as the destroyer of fundamental Islamic values and the Saudi government as their accomplices."

The rebels were eventually routed and their leader executed. But heed Lewis's point about what happened simultaneously. A demonstration in support of the rebels took place in the Pakistani capital of Islamabad. "A rumor had circulated – endorsed by (then-Iranian ruler Ruhollah) Khomeini – that American troops had been involved in the Mecca clashes. The American embassy was attacked by a crowd of Muslim demonstrators, and two Americans and two Pakistan employees were killed."

Why did Khomeini do this, other than the fact that he wasn't a nice guy? Simple. It was just one of many emerging, devious strategies – this one involving just a simple lie – in a new, evolving war against the American "Satan." Lewis writes, "Then, as in the past, this world of unbelievers was seen as the only serious force rivaling and preventing the divinely ordained spread and triumph of Islam."

The overall worldview against "the Great Satan" comes from Osama bin Laden himself, in a chilling May 28,

1998, interview with an ABC-TV reporter:

"We have seen in the last decade the decline of the American government and the decline of the American soldier, who is ready to wage cold wars and unprepared to fight long wars. This was proven in Beirut when the Marines fled after two explosions. It also proves they can run in less than 24 hours, and this was also repeated in Somalia... The youth were surprised at the low morale of the American soldiers ... After a few blows, they ran in defeat... They forgot about being the world leader and the leader of the new world order. (They) left, dragging their corpses and their shameful defeat, and stopped using such titles."

The radicals obviously view the U.S. as similar to the degenerate, decaying Roman Empire that was ripe for overthrow. It is the "decadence" of America that represents the greatest threat to their Islam. Sad to say, U.S. liberals don't understand this, nor do they understand that the presence of an Islamic fifth column in America – accepted and protected under "multiculturalism" – represents a grave danger in coming years as the Bush administration, and future administrations, pursue the war against *Islamic* terrorism.

When it comes to analyzing a domestic fifth column, aside from the problem of radicalism in all too many mosques, there is an additional factor that's cause for concern. The leader of the Christian-oriented Prison Fellowship Ministries warns it is "no accident that Islam is growing behind bars." Chuck Colson, in a 2002 a *Wall Street Journal* column, says: "Al Qaeda training manuals specifically identify America's prisoners as candidates for conversion."

Colson estimates one out of every six inmates in U.S. prisons is an adherent to Islam and the faith especially appeals to minorities. "Two million people occupy America's prisons and jails today – two-thirds of whom are non-white. Many feel oppressed by the white power structure..."

The clearly dangerous nexus here is that radical Islamists are preying on the disaffected, often using the guise of race, a hot-button issue covered in the first chapter.

Indeed, when many of these alienated ex-prisoners blend back into society, won't many inevitably want "payback"?

The Koran contains numerous passages that can incite followers to violence. Robert Spencer, author of *Islam Unveiled*, underscores this point: "When the Koran says, 'Slay the unbelievers wherever you find them. Arrest them, besiege them, and lie in ambush everywhere for them,' the extremists can point to that and many other verses of that kind and say: 'Look, this is what the religion teaches.'"

One would hope, too, that Islam's record just with regard to women will begin to separate thinking liberals and feminists who believe in Western-style civilized society from the mentality of the Dark Side. In this connection, Mark Steyn of Canada's *The National Post* speaks about an almost taboo subject: The increasing rape of Western women by Muslims in host countries. He cites Australia and Norway as examples of a growing trend.

Five days before Sept. 11, 2001, he notes, the Norwegian paper *Dagbladet* reported that 65 percent of the country's rapes were being committed by non-Westerners –

a category that in Norway is virtually all Muslim. Then consider Steyn's quote from a professor at the University of Oslo, who blandly explains that a reason for the disproportionate Muslim share of overall rapes was that in their native lands "rape is scarcely punished" because it is generally believed that "it is women who are responsible for rape."

As patriotic Americans inform themselves by adding up all of this information, no wonder that even one left-wing columnist – Ron Rosenbaum of the *New York Observer* – forced himself to reflect in a Nov. 25, 2002, column: "How can the Left be so blind as to who the real enemy is?" He admits to being amazed that his side of the political spectrum doesn't *get* that "the people who attacked us" don't just want God removed from some pledge, "they want to execute 'blasphemers,' beat women into burqas, stone gays – America was founded by escapees from such theocracies."

⌘ UNCHAINED TRUTH ⌘
FACTS, TALKING POINTS TO REMEMBER & USE

★ At its core, the widespread, radical strains of Islam are fundamentally at odds with Western culture. From its extreme practices regarding women and non-believers, radical Islam glorifies violence and demeans the individual.

☆ Radical Islam's clear message is hostile to Christianity, Judaism, Hinduism and other of the world's great religions.

☆ Every citizen, whether through a letter to the editor to their local newspaper or in a call to a radio talk show, should ask Muslim leaders in this country to condemn religious-sponsored terrorism. If President Bush's oft-repeated thesis is right – that Islam is basically a peaceful religion – then why are so few leading American Muslims and their "peaceful" brethren across the globe condemning the violence?

☆ Radical Muslims view the West as culturally inferior and morally bankrupt. Christian Arabs and moderate Muslims are especially despised. In the eyes of Osama bin Laden and others, today's terrorist efforts are Allah's vehicle to topple the "weak" democratic Western powers and Arab leaders who are U.S. allies.

☆ Radical Islam is a direct threat to the United States in terms of its aggressive recruitment of disaffected Americans, including prison-population minorities. By preying on the worst fears and darker angels of disaffected Americans, radical Muslims are creating a virtual army of supporters within our borders.

☆ The "war against terrorism" is, in fact, the latest manifestation of the ongoing war between freedom and tyranny. Radical Islam demonstrates a hatred of individual liberty, freedom of expression and speech, equality of persons under the law, and democratic values. Elected representatives at the national level need to be continually reminded of this from constituents.

★ In the interests of national security, the United States should not flinch from official "profiling" of individuals with ties to radical Islamic nations or groups. Rather than wasting billions of dollars, work hours, and disrupting the lives of millions of American citizens who never fit the terrorist "profile," the United States should focus its efforts on controlling our borders and closely monitoring those who enter them – especially if the individuals match the profile of suspected terrorists.

CHAPTER FOUR

FOREIGN POLICY
&
PROJECTING OUR MILITARY

THE LIBERAL LINE

The United States military-industrial complex seeks to project its immoral might and influence around the world for the profit and personal gain of those in power, including members of the current Bush administration. The U.S. should never act unilaterally regarding military force. U.S. armed forces should be subordinated to the United Nations, and human rights violations by our military personnel must come under the jurisdiction of an international criminal court. More U.S. foreign aid, especially to Muslim lands, will win their hearts and minds. Humanitarian assistance with U.S. money, which conservatives call "nation-building," should be the goal for poor nations. "Duty, honor and country" is an outmoded militarist slogan.

UNCHAINING THE TRUTH

Consider all of the amazing, revolutionary advances in U.S. weaponry and communications just since the dawn of the 21st century:

★ A Predator drone's deadly Hellfire missile, controlled by CIA computer operators in Florida, blows up a car filled with al Qaeda leaders on a faraway Yemen street.

★ Global Hawks, circling foreign skies, send back a stream of video images for military commanders.

★ A new Apache tank-killing helicopter stands ready to create havoc among our enemies.

★ The improved B-2 Stealth bomber can now drop sixteen 2,000-pound laser-guided bombs – better than anything we had in the 1991 Gulf War.

★ A house can be surgically obliterated, while leaving adjacent homes on the street intact, thanks to the latest Global Positioning System weapons.

★ Then there's that TV image of U.S. Special Forces soldiers armed with laptop computers on horseback chasing terrorists.

Incredible.

Military analysts say all the new precision weapons, coupled with better infrared sensors and communications gadgets, should make future wars quicker and less bloody for our side. But then there are the political and foreign policy equations – specifically when and how a U.S. president should unleash all of these superior armaments.

And, of course, there is the central question "why?"

which the American people and its elected representatives must always ask.

The Dark Side doesn't respect limited government, as documented in other chapters. But just as in domestic issues, a lot of confusion could be avoided in our foreign relations if we ask: What is the proper role of the federal government, as dictated by the Constitution?

The *right* answer is that the national government should serve to protect our people from any nation or terrorist who seek to do us harm. If this criteria is followed, there is a reason for U.S. action. Having said this, though, there will always be grey areas and grounds for healthy national debates like the ones that emerged in 2003 regarding Iraq and North Korea.

Using a "national interest first" standard, for example, one could argue endlessly about major U.S. interventions in recent decades from Vietnam to the 1991 Gulf War. At the same time, all notions of globalism like the oft-chided remark by former President George Bush about a "new world order," as well as needless projections of U.S. military power in the 1990s (Somalia, Haiti and the Balkans being prime examples), would be automatically rejected under this national interest standard.

Mark Sanford, a three-term congressman from South Carolina later elected governor of that state, wisely counseled, "If you or I were appointed commander-in-chief for a day and had to console a mother whose son had been killed in the line of duty, we would want to look that mother in the eye and say her son had not died in vain." He once told me "the central question in foreign policy is: Does it pass the mommy test?" Sanford's "test" also dictates that sending our troops abroad should be tied to the national interest and the chance to affect lasting change — "one without the other won't do." So to ensure that the son (or daughter) had not died in vain, we go back to using the "national interest first" standard while asking what is the mission and what are the exit strategies.

Pat Buchanan, often criticized by liberals and some conservatives as an 'isolationist," nevertheless makes a salient point in *A Republic, Not an Empire* when he instructs that "any true foreign policy must grow out of a nation's history and its heart. It cannot be grafted on; it must be organic and rooted in the nation's national interests." This concern is crucial to the ongoing debates of the 21st century. So when it comes to employing force with, say, a Stalinist backwater like North Korea – whose leader once vowed to turn the U.S. into "a sea of fire" – will a military response pass the "mommy test"? And will we be pursuing our foreign policy goals constitutionally?

For example, one of the most misguided and expensive projections of American military power occurred when President Bill Clinton ordered a U.S. bombing campaign against the sovereign state of Yugoslavia to force dictator Slobodan Milosevic to remove his forces from Kosovo – a part of Yugoslavia. The "defensive" North Atlantic alliance, of which the U.S. is a member, suddenly changed its mission in order to attack a country involved in a civil war (involving, by the way, radical Muslims).

The 1998 U.S. intervention cost U.S. taxpayers $3 billion – and resulted in an American occupation force in Kosovo to keep Muslims and non-Muslims from killing one another. Most importantly, Clinton's original ultimatum to Yugoslavia – to remove its forces from Kosovo or be attacked – never received congressional approval.

When one considers there are at least 70 civil wars and insurrections going on around the world annually, it should strike a reasonable observer as insane to think about committing U.S. forces into one of them – Yugoslavia-style – when the national interest is clearly not at stake. (Clinton even justified the bombing of Yugoslavia as a politically correct effort to "stop racism.")

Then there's the issue of our allies. Consider:

★ Since the Soviet Union collapsed, many Americans have wonder when our friends, especially our European ones and Canada, will begin to adequately provide and spend for their own defense. (And why can't NATO police its own Balkans backyard?)

★ When it comes to Israel, many Americans asked in 2003 why their country should agree to underwrite an additional $10 billion in loan guarantees to Prime Minister Ariel Sharon when he refused President Bush's call to pull the Israeli army out of the West Bank. Yes, the United States should help protect Israel's security. But we shouldn't help it build Jewish settlements in the West Bank and allow U.S. aid to help wage war on the Palestinian people (as opposed to Palestinian terrorists).

★ With regard to Iraq, our allies (especially ones in the Arab world) had to ask why the United Nations allowed Iraq for years to violate international accords and stockpile weapons of mass destruction until President Bush – with congressional approval – unilaterally began giving Saddam Hussein ultimatums in 2002-03.

The Bush administration's evolving war on terrorism appears both focused and nebulous. Certainly any analysis after the first anniversary of the Sept. 11 attacks should conclude that there were many successes. At the cost of just a few dozen U.S. casualties, the radical Islamic Taliban militia controlling Afghanistan, and who harbored al Qaeda terrorists, was defeated in a swift month-and-a-half war. Most governments around the world, ranging from neutral nations to hostile Arab states, helped arrest or foil al Qaeda killers.

Finally, the disruption or destruction of terror cells in North America, Europe and elsewhere continues on a seemingly regular basis.

Those inside and outside the Bush administration, however, who think we can militarily occupy Iraq or other Third World countries over a fairly long term, and hope such nations can then evolve into some sort of democratic enclaves, are hopelessly naïve. The great conservative thinker Russell Kirk counsels, "Various American voices have been raised ... to proclaim enthusiastically that soon all the world ... will embrace an order called democratic capitalism. It seems to be the assumption of these enthusiasts . . . that the political structure and the economic patterns of the United States will be emulated in every continent, for evermore."

This concept, Kirk warned a Heritage Foundation audience, is both liberal and "neoconservative" folly.

After all, there are hardly any Thomas Jeffersons or Adam Smiths coming to the fore in Iraq or anywhere else in the Third World.

Not to be forgotten, too, is that while many Democrats and liberals say they support the general concept of the war on terrorism, the hard Left openly and continually displays its visceral hatred of "Amerika" (as they derided our "Nazi-like" country during the Vietnam war).

At a January 18, 2003, "peace rally" in Washington, Dr. Ghazi Khaksan of the Council on American Islamic Relations actually offered greetings to a cheering throng in the name of the "Mujahideen," a term closely associated with al Qaeda terrorists.

WABC Radio's Curtis Sliwa also reported on the rally: "They were taking out their signs – 'Bush is the Evil One' and 'There's a Terrorist Behind Every Bush.' Out of the maybe 120 signs that I saw . . . [there wasn't] one pejorative placard demeaning Saddam Hussein." (My favorite sign, incidentally, was displayed on TV at a patriotic counter-demonstration: "If You Are Going To Burn Our Flag, Wrap Yourself In It!")

The usual Vietnam-era suspects were beating "antiwar" drums in 2002-03. Actress Jane Fonda, actor Ed Asner, film producer Oliver Stone, feminist Gloria Steinem, writer Gore Vidal and other prominent leftists signed a "Statement of Conscience" by a group they dubbed "Not In Our Name."

With regard to President Bush's policy to affect a "regime change" in Iraq, the group labeled it "unjust, immoral and illegitimate." The statement sounded the trumpet for Americans to "resist the war and repression that has been loosed on the world by the Bush administration." And the Dark Side fully emerges into the light of day when "Not In Our Name" declares it will "extend a hand to those around the world suffering from these policies ... in word and deed." That's an incredible pledge of support to America's enemies, as well as a blatant undermining of the American military who are fighting, or are poised to fight, our enemies.

When the U.S. military is committed to future battles, however, leftists and the internationalist elite in and outside our borders are planning a booby trap.

Imagine this scenario: A U.S. pilot given orders to bomb an Iraqi military installation inadvertently causes "collateral damage," killing civilians. He is hauled before an international court in the Netherlands on charges of committing "war crimes." The court convicts him and sentences him to life in prison.

Impossible? Not at all. In July 1998 in Rome a majority of United Nations member governments approved a treaty to create an International Criminal Court with powers to investigate, try and punish anyone who violates certain international human rights.

Thanks to massive grassroots opposition, both the Clinton and Bush administrations opposed the pact. But as prominent legal scholars Lee Casey and David Rivkin pointed out in a 1999 analysis, the global court may try to prosecute Americans anyway. "In an astonishing break with the accepted norms of international law, the Rome treaty would extend the ICC's jurisdiction to the citizens of the countries that have not signed and ratified the treaty," they wrote.

Any country that ratified the treaty should have received a reduction in U.S. foreign aid. But the bottom line is that an American president and Congress must never agree to honor a global court – an unlawful institution which violates the principles of self-government and popular sovereignty, and which confuses beyond recognition the oath taken by soldiers (including the Commander-in-Chief) to "preserve, protect and defend the Constitution" against "all enemies, foreign and domestic." Although I will be undoubtedly criticized for saying so, it is a uniquely American phenomenon to go into battle for an ideal as simple as "securing the blessings of liberty." The Dark Side would have American men and women passive during times of immediate threat, while policing the self-determined excesses of various and sundry local and regional conflicts across the globe.

The founder and co-editor of *The American Conservative*, Taki Theodoracopulos, offers a cogent follow-up: "Don't forget 1945. The West faced the same challenge back then in the Cold War with Stalin's Russia . . . The lesson of the Cold War was that a free, rich West could afford to face down poor, evil regimes over time."

Taki's point is well-taken – America's most powerful weapons may not be military in nature at all. But the proverbial 'tip of the spear' should be strong enough to back down the greatest threats to freedom – and that is, in fact, military in nature.

Should America be willing, nay, obligated to act unilaterally when its national interests are threatened? The clear answer is yes; who else at this stage of American global hegemony could do it? The Dark Side would have Americans, under U.N. command, policing whichever Third World local conflict happens to be the cocktail party topic of pitiable conversation in New York, Washington and Los Angeles salons.

The Dark Side would never, ever countenance military action under U.S. command against a direct threat to our nation's security. Why? For the same reason that "allies" like Germany and France knee-jerk their opposition to the expression of American military might: we seem like bullies when we lash out, for whatever purpose.

The "national interest first" approach, though, still provides ample room for debate and interpretation. Correctly or incorrectly, the current Bush administration boasts two distinct schools of thought on American interventionism, particularly regarding Iraq and even North Korea. The so-called "Powell Doctrine," loosely derived from then-Chairman of the Joint Chiefs of Staff Colin Powell during the Gulf War, ostensibly supports military action when the objective is clear, the American people are supportive, the force used is overwhelming, the timeline for engagement is short, and the exit strategy is clear – all under the banner of a "coalition," ostensibly to demonstrate unified world opinion. This school of thought is well-informed by the American experience in Vietnam, a conflict which – again, correctly or incorrectly – was lambasted as a "politician's war."

A seemingly competing school of thought in the current Bush administration is the so-called "Rumsfeld Doctrine," named for the current hard-nosed Defense Secretary. (Vice President Dick Cheney falls into the same camp.) In essence, the doctrine calls for the projection of military power as needed, with overwhelming force; however, in the case of the war on terrorism, the timeline and exit strategies may have to be worked out as we go. As to the need for a coalition of support for action, Rumsfeld has said, "The mission determines the coalition."

In a late 2002 address to a Hillsdale College dinner, columnist Charles Krauthammer described the "new unilateralism" as follows: "[America must] be guided by our own independent judgment, both about our own interests and about global interests . . . should we exercise prudence? Yes. There is no need to act the superpower in East Timor or Bosnia, as there is in Afghanistan or in Iraq. There is no need to act the superpower on steel tariffs, as there is on missile defense."

Krauthammer continued: "The prudent exercise of power calls for occasional concessions on non-vital issues, if only to maintain some psychological goodwill. There's no need for gratuitous high-handedness or arrogance . . . [however], countries will cooperate with us first our of their own self-interest, and second out of the need and desire to cultivate good relations with the world's unipolar power. Warm feelings are a distant third."

Krauthammer uses Yemen as an example: following the attack on the U.S.S. *Cole*, Yemeni officials hampered U.S. investigators at every turn – despite the fact that the Clinton administration was "obsessively" multilateralist. However, after the prosecution of a quick, technology-driven war waged on the orders of the current Bush administration in Afghanistan in which an uncooperative Muslim regime was thrown from power, the Yemenis are now active partners in the war on terrorism.

This underscores the point that concerted American military action, done with a clear purpose and waged in an overwhelming fashion, can turn reluctant governments into partners. But, as I have echoed here, such power must be demonstrated sparingly but effectively – and only toward the goal of protecting vital national interests.

There is also the old argument, trotted out again during the Bush administration, about whether there is ever a "just war." Rod Dreher, in a compelling *National Review* article, cleverly thought to interview U.S. military chaplains on this point. He interviewed Col. Vincent J. Inghilterra, who related he had stared into the face of evil more than once. Evil definitely exists, the 34-year Army veteran and Roman Catholic priest assured Dreher. "We (chaplains) have actually seen the oppression, the devastation, the hopelessness, the absolutely inexplicable, irrational hatred a person can have against another human being. It astounds me. ...There is only one way to deal with that evil, and that's to confront it, with force if necessary."

Dreher wrote that "the divide between military and civilian clergy over the Iraq war is philosophically deep." Naturally, many clergy in the civilian world just don't have their perspective. In this context, Dreher cited the view of Philip M. Hannan, the retired Catholic archbishop of New Orleans and a retired World War II chaplain. Hannan openly criticized fellow American bishops for their pacifist pronouncements on a war with Iraq, essentially saying that since the bishops had no experience with tyranny, they had no idea how to cope with it.

Dreher found that the clerical pacifism in "the civilian world" has left some members of the military confused, betrayed and even angry toward religion. Those soldiers, sailors and air force personnel ought to re-read Gen. Douglas MacArthur's inspiring speech of May 12, 1962, at the U.S. Military Academy at West Point. For that matter, his entire speech should be required reading for any American high school student taking a history course.

"Duty, honor, and country – those three hallowed words reverently dictate what you want to be, what you can be, what you will be. They are your rallying point to build courage when courage seems to fail, to regain faith when there seems to be little cause for faith, to create hope when hope becomes forlorn... The unbelievers will say they are but words, but a slogan, but a flamboyant phrase. Every pedant, every demagogue, every cynic, every hypocrite, every troublemaker, and, I am sorry to say, some others of an entirely different character, will try to downgrade them even to the extent of mockery and ridicule. (The general understood the Dark Side.) But these are some of the things they build. They build your basic character. They mold you for future roles as the custodians of the nation's defense. They make you strong enough to know when you are weak, and brave enough to face yourself when you are afraid."

MacArthur continued, "This does not mean you are warmongers. On the contrary, the soldier above all people prays for peace, for he must suffer and bear the deepest wounds and scars of war. But always in our ears ring the ominous words of Plato, that wisest of all philosophers: 'Only the dead have seen the end of war' ... The long gray line has never failed us. Were you to do so, a million ghosts in olive drab, in brown khaki, in blue and gray, would rise from their white crosses, thundering those magic words: duty, honor, country."

Let the political Left and their pacifist friends choke on those moving words.

♋♋ Unchained Truth ♋♋
Facts, Talking Points To Remember & Use

★ The United States is the lone world superpower. As such, we bear the responsibility to use our military effectively, powerfully, but with tremendous reluctance to enter into the dozens of local and regional conflicts around the world.

★ The "national interests first" approach to American military action means that intervention in places like Bosnia, Haiti, and Somalia breed rather than stop hatred for the U.S. and its interests. We must ask whether the goal is worth the price.

★ Liberals urge intervention by U.S. forces under U.N. command to police ethnic and religious conflicts around the globe. Yet, there is no example of any successful intervention by U.S. forces – whether under U.N. command or not – in any such conflict at any time. Some conflicts are simply beyond our reach to control them.

★ History tells us that perceived American weakness fosters bold actions and defiance from governments who seek to do us harm or resent American influence – World War II, Korea, and Vietnam each teach us important lessons in preparedness, willingness to act apart from world coalitions, and the critical point of *why we are fighting.*

★ American economic and social forces are often more effective than military forces at changing the hearts and minds of, and bankrupting, hostile governments. The Cold War is the perfect example.

★ American military strength must be used sparingly, judiciously, but with a clarity that does not confuse – the *threat* of American military action must be made only when it can and will be carried out. Delays, after threats of force, damage credibility and spur the "cowboy Americans" mentality.

★ Contrary to domestic pacifists and all too many in the liberal clergy, there is evil and there certainly can be "just" wars to combat it.

CHAPTER FIVE

THE WAR FOR OUR COURTS
THE LAST LINE OF DEFENSE
&
THE FIRST LINE OF LUNACY

THE LIBERAL LINE

The United States now comprises diverse people and cultures. As such, judges should have the power to change laws when circumstances dictate. The U.S. Constitution is a document in flux, and is many times irrelevant to modern society. Therefore, federal judges should be chosen on the basis of their views on issues, and should be tested on their ideologies. Tort reform is the last gasp of reactionary conservatives.

UNCHAINING THE TRUTH

We are a nation of laws, not of men. Our government is constitutional, not political. Our highest court is the arbiter of constitutional controversies, and the protector of unalienable rights. As former President Ronald Reagan underscored, "Freedom is indivisible – there is no 's' on the end of it. You can erode freedom, diminish it, but you cannot divide it and choose to keep 'some freedoms' while giving up others."

Ignoring the law, whether seen as politically expedient or ideologically sound, suggests that the courts are merely devices to be used to change policy. Al Gore openly proclaimed in a 1992 debate that "the Constitution is a living, breathing document ... intended by our founders to be interpreted in the light of the constantly evolving experience of the American people."

The courts, however, are partners with specific duties separate and apart from lawmaking and law execution. We've missed that point as a nation for too long, to our great peril.

As president of one of the nation's most aggressive constitutional public interest law firms, I am made aware on a daily basis that the "federal courts need fixing," as my Georgia friends say. Judge Robert Bork, President Ronald Reagan's Supreme Court nominee demonized in 1987 by liberals in a classic "litmus-testing" process, properly warned of the danger of the "political seduction of the law."

The important place that the law enjoys in American

political theory is grounded on public confidence. When citizens no longer believe in the impartiality of our judges and the legal processes they oversee, the carefully crafted system of checks and balances designed by our nation's Founding Fathers is in jeopardy.

Despite the blatantly false claim that a slender majority of politically-driven Supreme Court justices delivered up the presidency to George W. Bush against the wishes of the voters, most Americans appear to know better. But that could change.

The claim that politics, and not law, determined the outcome of the 2000 presidential election is constantly peddled by a vocal minority of leading leftists like Sen. Hillary Clinton, D-N.Y., Mary Francis Berry, the Clintonite chairwoman of the U.S. Civil Rights Commission, and Laurence Tribe, a Harvard law school professor.

Tribe testified before the U.S. Senate in June 2001, "With a Supreme Court that is already so dramatically tilted in a rightward direction, anything less than a concerted effort to set the balance straight would mean perpetuating the imbalance that gave us not only *Bush v. Gore,* but the myriad of decisions in the preceding half-dozen years in which the court thumbed its nose at Congress and thus the American people."

Sen. Charles Schumer, D-N.Y., actually announced on June 21, 2001, that Democrat members of the U.S. Senate should apply their own litmus test to judges nominated by President George W. Bush. Yet common-sense Democrats and Republicans continue to caution against this strategy. For example, in a conversation this author had with Sen. Arlen Specter, R-Pa., the liberal Republican stressed that litmus-testing had to be rejected for the good of the nation – and that he'd keep working with Sen. Joseph Biden. D-Del., to implement a system ensuring that judicial nominees, regardless of party, be given timely committee hearings and that the nominations would be sent to the full Senate for an up-or-down floor vote.

(Of course, many Senate Democrats want to pursue a strategy of "filibustering to death" Bush nominees who are particularly odious to them. Biden appears to be the only Judiciary Committee Democrat who might agree with Specter and other Republicans on such a plan –assuming Schumer & Co. don't ultimately dissuade him.)

Clinton administration lawyer Lloyd Cutler and senior Bush attorney C. Boyden Gray both condemn the ideological testing of judges.

"To make ideology an issue in the confirmation process [in which the U.S. Senate examines and confirms presidential nominees] is to suggest that the legal process is and should be a political one," Cutler says. "That is not only wrong as a matter of political science, it also serves to weaken public confidence in the courts."

It is difficult to conceive of a more wrong-headed, destructive approach to selecting those who will preside over our legal processes. In Schumer's case, his votes against Attorney General John Ashcroft and Solicitor General Ted Olson were based on his pet issues – gun control, abortion rights, race-based quotas, and zealous government regulation of the private sector.

Issue-based litmus-testing of judicial nominees was once decried by liberals when conducted by a few conservatives – as in the late 1960s when then-Sen. Strom Thurmond, R-S.C., filibustered against Supreme Court Chief Justice nominee Abe Fortas because of his leftist ideology. Consider, however, that by the time the 1980s rolled around, it was a Democratic-controlled U.S. Senate that scorched Judge Bork and personalized its attack in 1991 on Justice Clarence Thomas. –

In any case, and under any circumstances, litmus-testing of judicial nominees subjects the process to the transient nature of political issues rather than an examination of judicial temperament. In other words, what's 'in' in today's politics may be 'out' in a decade – and federal judges are appointed for life.

It is worth reiterating a truism about our system of government. The legislature – Congress – makes the laws. The executive branch – the President and his administration – enforce the laws. The courts interpret the laws.

Judicial activism disrupts this order by empowering and encouraging judges to legislate from the bench rather than interpreting what is required by the U.S. Constitution and the laws enacted by Congress. To paraphrase James Madison, the courts are to exercise not the will of men, but the judgment of law.

Not all political conservatives are judicially conservative, nor do we all support the concept of the judge as a legal referee rather than a player. Many conservatives would love to see the courts forbid abortion, thereby making new law. Many liberals would love to see the courts back away from vigorous enforcement of current laws against drug possession and mandatory sentencing of those convicted, thereby restraining the courts' powers. Simply put, many of the convenient political labels like "conservative" and "liberal" don't hold together when we consider the courts.

The nation's leading professional association of conservative attorneys, The Federalist Society, serves a key role in the process of reminding Americans (and especially students trapped in liberal-dominated law schools) how the courts matter to our daily lives. Federalist leaders are fond of repeating that judges should "hear courteously, answer wisely, consider soberly, and decide impartially."

The confidence of common-sense conservatism rests in the notion that *we are right on the issues.* Given a level playing field, and an impartial forum, our ideas will win – and liberty will be protected. As proponents of judicial restraint, we believe judges are not to use their office of trust as a platform to enact their own views on important matters of public debate. Judges need not compete with the constitutionally empowered Congress and chief executive for lawmaking privileges.

Consider the national outrage when two California federal judges declared the words "under God" in our nation's pledge of allegiance violate the vague concept of "separation of church and state." The public outcry, including a nearly unanimous bipartisan Congress, was deafening. Attorneys at Southeastern Legal Foundation, among others, raised arguments against the decision, citing case law precedent and the sense of the Founding Fathers that we are a nation that recognizes the existence of God and His vital activity in the affairs of men.

Nevertheless, the activist court cabal in California, followed by a denial of reconsideration by the full Ninth Circuit Court of Appeals, has sought to control the contents of the nation's Pledge. Public pressure was effective in this case, but in order to drive a nail into the coffin of irresponsible judicial lawmaking, this case should be heard by the U.S. Supreme Court. That is the effective "hammer" of the court system – the power to terminate bad law based on the U.S. Constitution and historical case law.

It is important to understand how our Anglo-American judicial system differs from all other systems in the world. In continental Europe, for example, judges serve as fact-finder and legal decision-maker. In our system, judges ensure fair play and dictate adherence to rules in the conduct of a trial – fact-finding and determining "truth" are left to juries of peers. In Europe, an individual accused of a crime bears the burden to show that he or she is innocent; here, the accused is guaranteed innocence until proven guilty by the prosecution.

Why are these differences important? Because the Anglo-American system alone among the world's legal systems recognizes the importance of the individual above the power of the government. In our system, the guardian of the judiciary's integrity is the judge.

In the civil cases against federal, state, and local gov-

ernments in which Southeastern Legal Foundation partici-
pates, on constitutional issues ranging from free speech and
private property rights, to affirmative action and government regulation of the private sector, the critical role of the
judge is to ensure that a single man, woman, or group has an
opportunity to be heard. In the face of the overwhelming
power and nearly unlimited resources of government defendants, the "little guy" deserves the chance to protect his or
her rights. Only in our system – and only when judges
understand their roles as defenders of the open system we
enjoy – can the little guy have the chance to shake the
world.

The list of social and economic seismic shifts in the
United States can ultimately be traced to the courts – not to
Congress or the president. Consider the demise of racial
segregation, or the end of unfair government "taking" of private property without just compensation, or barring government racial quotas for public contracts. In each instance, a
single person or group stood firm against an apparent tide of
government power. In each instance, because judges were
fair and impartial, the "little guy" won. That's how important
our judges have been, and that's why it's so important in the
future to have the right kind of judges (and lawyers, as offi-
cers of the court) to protect the right to be heard.

The wisdom of George Washington isn't extensively
taught in public schools anymore, but our first president was
highly familiar with what the founders intended: " (T)he
Constitution... till changed by an explicit and authentic act
of the whole people, is sacredly obligatory upon all." And,

he added for emphasis: "Let there be no change by usurpa-
tion ... it is the customary weapon by which free governments are destroyed."

One wonders what Washington and the other
Founding Fathers would think today, though, about the
reflections of the aforementioned Judge Bork, who splashes
some cold water of reality on lovers of liberty.

Writing in a Jan. 20, 2003, *Wall Street Journal* column,
the judge writes that "liberalism dominates the strategic
heights of our culture: the universities, media, churches,
Hollywood and the foundations. Liberalism's most powerful
position, arguably, is its dominance in the law."

Warming to the subject, Bork continues: "Judges on
both national and international tribunals have generally
aligned themselves with 'elite' classes that despise conservatism and its culture, and are thus well to the left of the general public. The result is not only the steady decline of self-
government and national sovereignty but also the pushing of
the culture to the left. Today's liberalism celebrates the liberation of the individual, but that liberation is only from the
traditional culture of the community, and from the laws that
reinforce it. The individual is not often liberated from the
demands of authoritarian liberalism, sometimes referred to,
though inadequately, as 'political correctness.'"

Bork concludes with a chilling observation:

"(Supreme Court) Justice Antonin Scalia accurately
describes the state of play: 'Day by day, case by case, (the
Supreme Court) is busy designing a Constitution for a country I do not recognize.'"

Yet, in spite of this "state of play," Bork and others battling the Dark Side (including key players within the Bush administration) hold out hope for some type of positive change in an important area – tort reform. It should be the battle cry of Americans fed up with exorbitant judgments and the manner in which they are distributed. (The lawsuits the tobacco companies settled with the states is Exhibit A.)

Peter Angelos, the tort lawyer who sought a $1 billion fee from Maryland for his tobacco work (and who eventually settled for $125 million) later sued cell phone manufacturers. There was no injury to the plaintiffs. But simply because his plaintiffs worry that there might be some future medical problem due to using the phones, they want the manufacturers to pay the costs of monitoring their health. Incredible!

Another example of the "law of unintended consequences" resulting from huge class-action lawsuits is with asbestos. In the first few rounds of class-action settlements, the major manufacturers have been bankrupted, while thousands of individuals have received millions of dollars in payments. Due to crazy "fault" determinations by various judges, who may not have foreseen the extent of the health crisis resulting from asbestos, there is little or no money left for the tens of thousands of individuals who now seek – or may soon seek – payments. In this case, "tort reform" is better called "judicial reform."

Consider, too, the results of various state court decisions on private sector decision-making. In Georgia, for example, the state Supreme Court rightly rejected a plaintiff's appeal to raise the standard of care required by banks that offer ATM services. In the case, an individual was attacked at an ATM, despite the fact that the bank offered a well-lighted facility and a guard on the premises. The plaintiff and his attorneys sought a heightened standard for all banks.

The result, as Southeastern Legal attorneys argued, would have been that banks would have simply closed ATM facilities in areas where potential crimes might have occurred to avoid potential problems. Entire communities, dependent on banks and financial service providers to sustain local businesses, would have suffered as a result.

And what about the lawsuits themselves?

Some states in which trial lawyers, who are major political contributors, exercise control over legislatures have allowed for so-called "venue shopping." This allows a plaintiff to pick the jurisdiction in which a lawsuit may be brought, which brings discredit to the entire justice system when it appears that forum-shopping is allowed.

For example, a contractor working on a project for an electrical company based in County A, who works on a job for the company in County B, is hurt on the job. The contractor chooses to sue the company due to alleged negligence in providing a faulty tool. Under traditional rules of venue, the contractor might be able to sue in County A, where the company is based, or in County B, where the alleged injury occurred. Under liberal venue-shopping rules, the contractor might instead sue in County C, where he or she lives, and which has absolutely no connection to the company or the place where the alleged injury occurred.

In theory and, as played out time and again to the detriment of our system, the employee's home county (and court) is much friendlier to the employee and much more hostile to the employer.

This cynical approach to our court system is nothing short of abuse. The result – companies are less likely to hire contractors and perform services outside their home base, for fear of risking potentially costly lawsuits.

Do Americans want a world in which manufacturers are held liable for others' irresponsible or criminal use of their products, and a world in which cities or counties sue on behalf of themselves to "protect" people? State laws should be strengthened that restrict government litigation against firms when products are misused by consumers. Court awards should be returned to taxpayers, minus reasonable attorney fees. That's a good first step in serving justice and controlling the predatory ambitions of trial lawyers.

Further, the mere threat of litigation, which causes many companies to simply settle the "dispute" for huge sums and pass those sums along to consumers, is enough to cause measurable ripples in our nation's economy. No proposal should infringe on the ability of an American to seek justice. But we must take the incentive out of litigation against companies – ranging from fast-food producers to gun manufacturers – that benefit trial lawyers and government.

UNCHAINED TRUTH

FACTS, TALKING POINTS TO REMEMBER & USE

★ The Anglo-American judicial system is the only system in the world that guarantees the rights of the individual over the power of the state.

★ The American judicial system works when judges are impartial, and fails utterly when they are not. James Madison said the courts are to exercise not the will of men, but the judgment of law.

★ Issue-based litmus-testing of federal judicial nominees – whether by the Democrats or by the Republicans – defeats the purpose of an impartial judiciary by making politicians out of judges.

★ Judges should interpret laws, not invent new laws which do not comport with the slow-moving system of common law (case law precedent) – which means honoring the U.S. Constitution's original intent.

★ In the American judicial system, the "little guy" is often the catalyst for major change – unlike the rest of the world. Thus, the impartiality of judges is critical to the process that allows the "little guy" to stand up to the powers of government.

★ Politically partisan "litmus-testing" of judicial nominees subjects the process of selecting judges to the changing whim of issue politics – and ultimately destroys public confidence in the third branch of government.

★ "Tort reform," in its various manifestations, is a basic viewpoint that individuals should ultimately be responsible for the results of their own conduct. The courts, on the other hand, should be a legitimate referee when legal harm is done. Instead, the courts have become the social "go-to" for every perceived "wrong," raising the question as to exactly what are the "rights" of Americans protected by the U.S. Constitution. Not every perceived wrong is a violation of someone's rights.

★ According to leading economists, the American economy now pays nearly 2 percent of the gross national product for runaway court verdicts and lawsuit-avoidance – a staggering amount in the hundreds of billions of dollars that threatens millions of jobs, the overall health of our economy, and the critical confidence that Americans must have in the integrity of the judicial system in order for it to work as envisioned by our founders.

CHAPTER SIX

TAXES, BIG GOVERNMENT
&
PROFIT

THE LIBERAL LINE

In America, there are the "rich," who control the big institutions of our society – corporations, institutions and, alas, government. The "rich," therefore, are the powerful. The rest of America, the "working poor," "middle class," and "working Americans," deserve a share of the power because, after all, America is a democracy. Taxes can encourage "good" behavior, like taxing cigarettes and gasoline; encouraging less use; taxes also fund the various programs needed by the "poor," paid for by those Americans who can most afford it – the rich.

UNCHAINING THE TRUTH

The claim by government on more and more of an individual's "wealth," which means any money an individual might have at any given time, is constantly and maddeningly applauded by the Dark Side. Liberals have traditionally and forcefully carried the day on taxation, from defining "rich" and "poor" to "fair" and "equitable." Step one for conservatives is to redefine the terms of the debate.

Consider "rich" and "poor." According to Americans for Tax Reform, a "rich" American (under the liberal definition) is anyone who earns more than $50,000 per year and supports a family of four. Understanding that today's cost-of-living requires a U.S. average of $48,000 in income for a family of four to own a home, maintain two automobiles, and feed and clothe the family, it is basically unfathomable that a family of four earning $50,000 in annual income would ever consider itself "rich."

The "poor," on the other hand, consist of non-working and working Americans who earn less than $50,000 per year and support a family of four.

But "poor" is also a broader class of people – according to liberals. Those Americans who are "historically disadvantaged," as described by the National Association for the Advancement of Colored People, include America's 34 million African-Americans, some 34 million Hispanic immigrants (legal and illegal), women (half the U.S. population), native Americans, the unemployed, and the homeless, constitute the "poor" for whom the government owes taxpayer benefits. In such instances, actual "wealth" has little or nothing to do with whether an individual is deemed "poor" by liberals – and the more than 600 programs funded by the federal government as "domestic aid" attest to the outrageous imbalance.

In short, for liberals, the American tax system is a means to control economic activity and to redirect resources to one group from another. No wonder 67 percent of high school seniors who were asked where the statement, "From each according to his ability, to each according to his need," thought that it was from the U.S. Constitution!

In fact, the statement came from Karl Marx, the self-avowed "enemy of capitalism" and father of communism, but the point is made – most Americans accept the basic definitions of socialized liberalism when it comes to our economic freedom.

As a result, the American tax system is designed to punish those who earn the most money – you know, "the rich." Of the $1.991 trillion paid in taxes in fiscal year 2001, approximately 50 percent came from individual income taxes, or roughly $994 billion. Of that amount, consider these startling facts:

• American families with income of $200,000 per year and over (2.7 percent if the population) paid 49.7 percent of the total income taxes.

• American families with income of $100,000 to $200,000 per year (9 percent of the population) paid 23.9 percent of the total income taxes.

• American families with income of $75,000 to

$100,000 per year (9.1 percent of the population) paid 11.6 percent of the total income taxes.

• Finally, American families with income of $50,000 to $75,000 per year (15.4 percent of the total population) paid 10.6 percent of the total income taxes. (Remember that income below $50,000 per year is considered "poor" by many liberal economic advocates).

Final tally: 11.7 percent of the U.S. taxpaying population pays 73.6 percent of total federal income taxes. 20.8 percent of the U.S. taxpaying population pays 85.2 percent of total federal income taxes. And, 36.2 percent of the U.S. taxpaying population pays 95.8 percent of total federal income taxes.

More startling is that, of the remaining 50 percent of taxes other than on income paid to the federal government (Social Security/Medicare, corporate income, estate, and excise taxes), 90 percent of these taxes are paid by less than 10 percent of the U.S. taxpaying population – an additional $897 billion per year.

The oft-cited Tax Foundation's "Tax Freedom Day," which represents the day of the calendar year through which taxpaying Americans must work to pay the total sum of taxes, was April 27 in 2002.

Here's what that tax burden represents:

Americans work an average of 51 days to pay federal, state and local income taxes, and another 29 days to pay social insurance programs like Social Security and Medicare. Sales and excise taxes represent another 18 days of work. Local property taxes represent an additional 11 days of work, followed by 8 days of work to pay for corporate income taxes. As a total, Americans now work longer to pay for government (approximately 117 days) than we will for food, shelter and clothing combined (approximately 106 days).

Think about it for a moment, and ask yourself a couple of questions: What is "economic freedom," and what does it mean?

To be sure, our nation's Constitution sets forth specific duties for our federal government, duties that must be paid for by the shared resources of our people. But in terms of the constitutional mandates, these duties are fairly limited – defense, postal service, the justice system and courts, the Congress, and the Chief Executive. Everything else – and I mention this with a nod to my Libertarian Party colleagues – is extra, based on changing political trends, a traditionally spendthrift Congress and chief executive, and the will (or lack thereof) of the American people.

One of the key architects of modern free enterprise, John Stuart Mill, pointed out that economic freedom is the lynchpin of individual liberty:

"A people may want a free government, but if, from insolence, or carelessness, or cowardice, or want of a public spirit, they are unequal to the exertions necessary for preserving it; if they will not fight for it when it is directly attacked; if they can be deluded by the artifices used to cheat them out of it; if by momentary discouragement or temporary panic, or a fit of enthusiasm for an individual they can be induced to lay their liberties at the feet of even a great man, or trust him with powers which enable him to subvert their institutions; in all these cases they are more or less unfit for liberty; and though it may be for their good to have had it even for a short time, they are unlikely long to enjoy it."

The bottom line: people are only as free as the government to which they give power allows them to be. Government control of individual economic status – the amount of money you earn and keep – can be no less coercive than some low-life holding a gun on a store cashier.

Freedom is a hollow shell without the means to enjoy and expand it. That's why a responsible expose´ of the American tax and economic condition must also include a review of its architects and their plans for a "controlled economy."

Ever heard of Norman Thomas? He was a six-time Socialist candidate for president. He never, of course, got elected under his own party banner but by the end of his political career Thomas was a happy man. He predicted that Keynesian economics, named after British Fabian economist John Maynard Keynes, "would be especially important" by the 1960s because it "represents a decisive break with laissez-faire capitalism."

It was a decisive break. And what is especially galling to those who cherish the Constitution and the Founding Fathers' love of Adam Smith economics is that this big government, big-spending, high-tax philosophy was embraced after World War II by leading Democrats and Republicans alike – Presidents Franklin Roosevelt, Lyndon Johnson and Richard Nixon being among the principal proponents.

Thomas lived to see his economic theories used as a vehicle for buying the votes and support of the masses with their own money! He even farsightedly wrote that "the American people probably will never knowingly accept socialism, but in the name of liberalism they will adopt every fragment of the socialist program."

Many latter-day politicians bristle at the charge of being socialistic, but under its basic definition – the sharing of all earned income by those who did not help earn it – they are squarely in the camp of socialism, if not Marxism.

The ghost of Keynes is no doubt elated that his big government/big spending policies are now being skillfully blended with the Dark Side's propaganda of hate, fear and class conflict.

Conservatives in and out of government – with Ronald Reagan as one of their more effective leaders – have tried to speak out and fight against the increasing rate of federal spending that has generated so many socialistic programs. But perhaps it was the late H.L. Mencken who best put the planners of socialism into proper perspective. Writing in the March 1936 *American Mercury*, the editorialist thundered, "On one point only did the Roosevelt planners and brain trusters appear to agree, and that was on the point that any man who worked hard at some useful task, husbanded his money prudently, and tried to provide some security for his old age and some heritage for his children was a low and unmitigated scoundrel."

How true that observation still is today. For socialists ranging from Franklin Roosevelt's planners to their big-spending contemporaries in both parties in Congress have an inherent hatred for individual reliance and private enterprise – despite pious declarations to the contrary.

Income distribution programs – which pushed federal government spending to far over half of the nation's Gross National Product – are fostering the Keynesian goal of a controlled economy. So the big question looms: Can this trend ever be reversed? If the Congress does not hold down, and slash, many federally-funded programs – and if the American taxpayer doesn't demand it – Mencken's American free enterpriser could just about be beaten by 2010.

Socialist California provides an example of how the entire nation could end up. A frank 2002 year-end news report in the San Jose *Mercury-News* was titled "California leads the way on the road to financial ruin." It says the governor and legislature "created a fiscal mess more than 20 times worse than anything Congress could manufacture," noting that "public investment is good rhetoric but, in practice, it doesn't necessarily ensure the needed revenue stream."

The paper chronicled the story of how climate-friendly California in the early and mid-1990s was once business-friendly, that land was cheap for a time, state services were good and the tax structure wasn't viewed as punitive. But, the report complains, the state "attracted immigrants, many of them undocumented, who drain public services... Lawmakers spent for schools, health care and highways and increased state hiring 15 percent." (It also noted "that other 'mega-states' such as Florida and Texas, with less generous government programs, proportionately smaller work forces and no income tax, are much better off. Their income is based on sales taxes, which might not be progressive, but their revenues have been more reliable.")

Then came the newspaper's jolting warning to other states and the nation:

"Class warriors who think the rich 'should pay their fair share' and favor high income and capital-gains taxes might want to consider what happened in California, where the top 10 percent of taxpayers provided 75 percent of the state's revenue. The stock market losses hit the wealthiest hardest, leading to a steep drop in state revenues... And it's only going to get worse. The deficit is going to require even more taxes and cuts that will renew the vicious cycle, making the state even less attractive."

Of course, blithely ignoring the California crisis, the Dark Side relentlessly pushes attacks on "the rich" and "the profit motive." They are aided by the many socialists teaching in the economics departments at most of the major American colleges and universities.

There are positive trends, however small. The conservative movement has carried the debate on so-called "death taxes," or those taxes levied on individual's estates when they die. Death taxes, as the name implies, have for decades wiped out family savings and property holdings, including family farms and small businesses. By framing the public debate and "owning" the title, conservatives are winning the hearts and minds of Americans who, above all, favor "fairness." Today, 70 percent of Americans favor complete repeal of the federal estate tax.

How can it be fair to tax the final tally of an individual's economic life? More importantly, as Congress properly determined several years ago, the federal government must wean itself from the billions of dollars in theft-by-taking achieved from stealing inheritances – some $23 billion collected in 1998 alone (less than 1 percent of the total federal revenue).

The current "death tax" plan in place allows for a "lifetime exclusion" of $675,000, followed by a tax rate of 37 percent up to $3 million, at which point the tax rate is 55 percent. The exemption is currently scheduled to increase in uneven amounts to $1 million in 2006. The death taxes "due" to the federal government must be paid 9 months after death, and must be paid in cash. The "death tax" was instituted in 1916 to help fund American efforts up to and including World War I and, as with most federal taxes and programs, has never been decommissioned.

However, with overwhelming public opposition to death taxes, based in large measure on effective public relations campaigns by such groups as 60 Plus, the Tax Foundation, the National Taxpayers Union, and Americans for Tax Reform, Congress and President George W. Bush will be hard-pressed *not* to act decisively to end this obnoxious tax immediately. That's what's meant by *"taking back our nation!"*

And let it be said, too, that the courts can play a vital role in rolling back unfair and, in some cases, unconstitutional taxes and fees. My organization, a constitutional public interest law firm, successfully attacked an illegal tax in the courts several years ago. At issue was a 50-year old "intangibles" tax on out-of-state stocks and bonds that cost Georgia taxpayers approximately $60 million a year. If you owned stock in Coca-Cola, a Georgia-based company, you paid no taxes on your holdings; if, however, you owned PepsiCo stock, a company based in North Carolina, you were compelled to pay state taxes on that holding. Unfair, yes; illegal, to be sure.

After bringing suit in Georgia, the Southeastern Legal Foundation educated state lawmakers as to the likely outcome of the case. The so-called commerce clause of the Constitution, as interpreted over the years by the U.S. Supreme Court, holds that similarly situated commercial interests must be treated the same, as interstate commerce must be allowed to flourish.

During the course of the litigation, a lawsuit from North Carolina challenging a similar state law made its way to the U.S. Supreme Court. Georgia lawmakers got the message – in no fewer than three bills, passing nearly unanimously through the General Assembly, the Georgia intangibles tax was repealed.

Never underestimate the power of good public relations on the right issue combined with a "tangible" legal issue raised in court!

But minor victories here and there across the American economic landscape do not, by themselves, erase decades of indoctrination about the "poor" and "rich," what constitutes "wealth," and what is "fair" for "working

Americans." Each and every announced candidate for the Democratic presidential nomination in 2004 has made as a centerpiece economic policies that focus on "benefits for working Americans" and "middle-class tax relief that doesn't benefit the rich" – code phrases that conservatives and a growing number of Americans are understanding to mean higher taxes, more government programs, and less individual economic independence.

Finally, some reflections on how the Dark Side always tries to make "profit" a dirty word. I remember when then-Carter administration advisor Alfred Kahn actually labeled as "obscene" a routine national corporate earnings report. Liberals like him ought to visit a Junior Achievement program. Businesses sponsor a student group which raises a small amount of capital to promote a product which it manufactures or markets, pays for raw materials and labor, pays taxes, uses advertising and then – if successful – declares dividends. Is this "obscene?"

Without profit, the free economy which conducts research, promotes mass demand through advertising, uses that mass demand for mass production and lower prices, creates jobs and pays taxes – all that would be impossible!

Who pays the high wages? The profitable companies. Who pays the low salaries? Those without a reasonable volume of profit.

Forbes founder B.C. Forbes once said those who waste capital or commit fraud are among the greatest enemies of capitalism. So remember that all the hot air and bad press about the Enron scandal or other corporate wrongdoing is not an indictment of free enterprise but a reminder of plain old human weakness.

Remember, too, there's good news for the future. *The Wall Street Journal* reports businesses are utilizing just a fraction of the technology currently available. Therefore, as they use more of this technology, productivity growth will keep rising – hiking incomes and profits. That's the best recipe for wealth creation. And, as many economists on our side underscore, productivity is the engine that drives our free enterprise system.

⌒⌒ UNCHAINED TRUTH ⌒⌒
FACTS, TALKING POINTS TO REMEMBER & USE

★ The liberal definition of "rich" and "poor" is cockeyed – the "rich" are families of four who earn $50,000 or more.

★ For liberals, the U.S. tax system is a Keynesian means to control the economy and redistribute wealth to one favored group over another.

★ Educate your friends and co-workers about "Tax Freedom Day," the day of the year through which U.S. taxpayers must work to pay the total sum of taxes (April 27 in 2002).

★ California is a prime example of how socialism destroys an economy – people leave, profit is discouraged, and taxes go up on those remaining to pay for a myriad of services.

★ The "death tax" – how can it be fair to tax the final tally of an individual's economic life and legacy? Remember that high taxes are due from estates – in cash – 90 days from the date of death. That kills family property, like farms, where the "value" is measured in real estate.

★ Profit is not a dirty word. Who pays the high wages? A profitable company. Who pays the low salaries? Those without a reasonable volume of profit.

CHAPTER SEVEN

UNMASKING THE ENVIRONMENTAL MOVEMENT

THE LIBERAL LINE

Environmentalism is a sound, science-based movement, with responsible leaders who struggle against irresponsible U.S. corporations who freely pollute our air, water, and earth. Environmentalists face daunting odds as they try to tell the truth about the earth's desperate situation, stifled as they are by the public relations machines of corporate America. The earth truly does "hang in the balance," as global warming, loss of rainforests, and pillaging of the earth's natural resources spell doom for humankind unless drastic action is taken. American consumers buying an SUV are anti-safety and anti-environment.

UNCHAINING THE TRUTH

Let's be clear about one thing – science and environmentalism are two very different animals. In fact, time and again, objective and credible scientific studies demonstrate that the environmental movement is merely political, not scientific.

Nature abhors a vacuum, and so does politics. The U.S. Environmental Protection Agency, a designated federal watchdog, consistently fails to convey accurate scientific evidence to its congressional overseers and the public, leaving a gaping hole in the public perception of America's current "clean" air and water status.

Into that gaping hole are rushing the nabobs of environmental politics – U.S. Public Interest Research Group, the National Environmental Trust, the Sierra Club and their allies. Taking advantage of the EPA's lack of focus and glacial-paced reform of regulatory programs responsive to the latest in scientific evidence, the fast-moving agenda-driven groups have seized the public's imagination. According to recent surveys, Americans believe that our air and water are getting worse – despite clear evidence to the contrary.

The EPA's inability and, in some cases, deliberate intent not to convey the best scientific results – even from its own Office of Research and Development – underscores the structural problems with the agency. Administrator Christie Todd Whitman noted the problem in her budget prioritization for 2002, requesting increased funding for the EPA's Science Advisory Board basic research. Her stated goal is to make the EPA a clearinghouse for accurate, timely scientific evidence regarding air, water, and ground quality. With 30 years' of regulatory dominance by attorneys and emphasis on short-term goals, the EPA's reformation will be slow in coming.

And, where leadership is lacking, conflict is sure to follow. There are currently more than forty major federal environmental lawsuits involving the EPA, which has joined the energy, chemical, and construction industries as prime targets for headline-seeking environmental groups. At stake is more than $1 trillion in combined potential damages, to say nothing of the millions in taxpayer funds spent to defend against sometimes-baseless claims.

U.S. PIRG's "take-no-prisoners" approach to public policy has particularly muddied the waters. Consider recent "reports," citing questionable scientific methodology, with explosive titles such as "Death, Disease, and Dirty Power;" "Darkening Skies;" and "Children At Risk." Funded almost entirely by the Pew Charitable Trusts, U.S. PIRG proudly portrays its throwback status in articles like, "Revitalizing the Spirit of the 60s."

In the absence of solid, clear statements from the EPA, U.S. PIRG and others are polluting the public market-place of ideas.

By admission, the EPA is not a scientific body. Its mandate is broad, covering air quality, water quality, land use issues, wetlands regulations, Endangered Species Act partial enforcement, chemical production, distribution and use, and energy waste disposal. Whitman's lobbying efforts to estab-lish and strengthen a core integrated research program is equally broad, aiming for the EPA to acquire chemical, biological, geological, social and economic understanding of environmental systems and their effect on humans.

While the EPA is not a total failure, given its sweeping responsibilities, the agency has trouble communicating its findings when it has them. A 2002 report from the National Legal Center for the Public Interest, *"Cartoon Science: The Struggle Between Politics and Science at the Environmental Protection Agency,"* lays out the case in clear terms.

Consider that the EPA recently reported that emissions of six principal air pollutants are down 31 percent since 1970, while electric generation (of which a large percentage is coal- generated) has increased 45 percent in that time.

The EPA, for example, reported lead pollution was reduced by 97 percent over a 23-year period. Carbon monoxide pollution fell 68 percent during that same time frame. (For anyone interested, the Pacific Research Institute has collected similar data chronicling this trend.)

But the EPA's good news never met the light of day. U.S. PIRG and its allies swamped the agency's information with a controversial "study" conducted by Abt Associates, which linked the operation of coal-fueled power plants with alleged airborne sulfate health problems. Widely reported in the general media, the Abt report nevertheless failed to follow accepted scientific methodology and peer review. An April 2002 review by The Annapolis Center's scientific and medical team revealed that the Abt study's "claims of linkages between operating power plants in the U.S. and community ill health lack scientific support."

So where can Americans – including those in Congress – turn for scientifically valid information on the status of our environment? The answer is clear: the millions of consumers, outdoors enthusiasts, homeowners, and employees of industries targeted by the radical environmentalists, *should* be able to trust the EPA. Yet until a top-down culture change and refocus of priorities occurs, the EPA will continue to be the weakest link in the national environmental debate.

And where does science meet science in a head-to-head battle of opinions? One of the juiciest and most controversial "environmental" subjects today is the phenomenon known as "global warming." A big win for common-sense conservatives and the majority of scientists who study global energy use and its effects on the environment came when the U.S. Senate declined to consider the Kyoto Protocol, an international treaty banning or greatly reducing the amount of energy-based toxins emitted by producers in the United States and western Europe.

The Kyoto Protocol would have slashed the ability of Western powers to continue the use and development of safer and more environmentally sound means of burning fuel – but the economic impact would have been devastating. U.S. government economic studies place Kyoto's cost to cut carbon dioxide emissions in the U.S. alone between $100 billion and $400 billion per year.

But what environmental benefit would these terrible cuts produce? According to many scientific experts, absolutely none. Why? Because Kyoto called for carbon reductions in developed nations but virtually no cuts in the very Third World countries who will add the most new sources of carbon to the atmosphere.

Communist China and Mexico, by the way, will become the world's leading polluters in the next few years. The environmentalist agenda appears to have a political, rather than "good earth," overtones.

The Dark Side of the environmentalist lobby is long on hype and scare tactics, and short on solutions, science and technology. It would never, for example, propose the most logical – and carbon-free—solution for the world's energy future: nuclear energy. A book could be written on that subject alone. But back to the "science" of global warming.

Dr. Sallie Baliunas, an astrophysicist at the Harvard-Smithsonian Center for Astrophysics, points out that no human-made global warming effects can be detected based on today's technology – and she represents the majority of truly scientific thought on this subject.

She emphasizes in a Hillsdale College speech that "in light of some of the hysterical language surrounding the issue of greenhouse gases, it is also worth noting that carbon dioxide, the primary . . . gas produced by burning fossil fuels, is not a toxic pollutant. To the contrary, it is essential to life on earth. And plants have flourished – agricultural experts estimate a ten percent increase in crop growth in recent decades – due directly to the fertilization effect of increased carbon dioxide in the air."

Dr. Baliunas points out that the environmentalists are

pushing the Kyoto agenda in part because it represents a "precautionary principle," that "doing something is promoted as insurance against possible risk to the earth." Her conclusion: "in the case of human-made global effects, the risk, premium and outcomes cannot be well-defined." In non-scientific parlance, the global warming gang is on the wrong foot, with the wrong agenda.

But why the effort at "the sky is falling, the sky is falling" if there is no science to suggest that global warming is an immediate threat to life on earth? The truth is in the funding.

Far from being a downtrodden bunch, they are well-funded, well-versed in the public relations tactics of the civil and women's rights movements, and can bend public opinion with questionable "polling" data and other tricks of the trade. A word to the wiser Americans who call themselves conservative – don't be fooled.

The worldwide environmentalist movement, exemplified by the coordinated efforts of the Green Party apparatus in the U.S. and western Europe, supports a one-world, statist agenda that is anathema to individual liberty. In order to illustrate this point without sounding too 'alarmist,' consider Former Vice President Al Gore's oft-criticized 1992 book, *Earth in the Balance: Ecology and the Human Spirit*. The 'tree-hugger tome' presents a lengthy ideological blueprint for the environmentalist political agenda. Gore makes clear that autonomous nation-states and industrialization, supported by "conservative" (meaning "Judeo-Christian") politicians and theologians, jeopardize not only his vague concept of "the environment," but also threaten human spiritual well-being:

> "The spiritual sense of our place in nature . . . can be traced to the origins of human civilization. A growing number of anthropologists and archeo-mythologists. . . argue that the prevailing ideology of belief in prehistoric Europe and much of the world was based on the worship of a single earth goddess, who was assumed to be the fount of all life and who radiated harmony among all living things. . . . [Ceremonial sites] seem to confirm the notion that a goddess religion was ubiquitous throughout much of the world until the antecedents of today's religions--most of which still have a distinctly masculine orientation--swept out of India and the Near East, almost obliterating belief in the goddess. The last vestige of organized goddess worship was eliminated by Christianity . . . .
>
> [I]t seems obvious that a better understanding of a religious heritage preceding our own by so many thousands of years could offer us new insights . . . ." (page 260)

Apart from the New Age-driven rhetoric of the "interconnectedness of all things," which provides a religious purpose to the environmental movement, the practical political agenda in Gore's book is no less radical in tactics and state-centered in ambition than Hitler's *Mein Kampf* or Mao's *Red Book*:

> "Adopting a central organizing principle – one agreed to voluntarily – means embarking on an all-out effort to use every policy and program, every law and institution, every treaty and alliance, every tactic and strategy, every plan and course of action – to use, in short, every means to halt the destruction of the environment . . . .

Minor shifts in policy, moderate improvement in laws and regulations, rhetoric offered in lieu of genuine change—these are all forms of appeasement, designed to satisfy the *public's desire to believe that sacrifice, struggle and a wrenching transformation of society will not be necessary.*" (page 274, Emphasis added)

As the fable writer Aesop observed, "We often give our enemies the means of our own destruction." Nowhere can this be seen more clearly than in the litigation-frenzied world of corporate America, where industrial giants and their charitable foundations provide tens of millions of dollars a year to radical environmental groups bent on tearing down the very institutions funding them.

The question is, why do corporations and foundations give to those who would destroy them? The main answer: To protect themselves against the inevitable next wave of costly, image-shattering "environmental" litigation.

Jesse Jackson's Rainbow/PUSH Coalition and its "special projects," such as the Citizenship Education Fund, have come under fire for soliciting tax-deductible contributions from corporations against whom he promised to "campaign" on alleged employment diversity issues. Wishing to avoid the ever-present klieg lights that accompany Rev. Jackson's press conferences, many corporations have given in – to the tune of tens of millions of dollars. As public scrutiny focuses on Jackson's self-serving agenda, a handful of corporations have thankfully begun defying his implied threats and taken public relations steps to gird for the inevitable "discrimination" battle.

The environmental movement has taken the same approach to corporate blackmail. By utilizing sophisticated political strategies involving direct lobbying efforts, public opinion surveys based on headline-grabbing "junk science," and the constant churn of court cases based on the Clean Air and Water Acts and federal wetlands statutes, environmentalists have developed a formula for success.

By implied threats of litigation, based on pseudo-scientific "studies" mentioned herein, radical environmental groups extort "grants" from energy and industrial corporations to fund their activities. The cost of the new taxes, fees, and regulatory "reform" advocated by these groups is ultimately paid by the American consumer.

In many instances, energy companies and alleged industrial "polluters" are not even the direct defendants in litigation; the U.S. Environmental Protection Agency and the various state environmental agencies are. The "moving" standards of air quality involving rates of particulate matter, carbon dioxide, sulfur dioxide, and nitrogen oxide emissions, argued and won in the various legislatures, provide ample questions about acceptable levels for courts to consider.

Air and water quality are much better today than they were 25 years ago, and better overall than a decade ago. Nevertheless, as standards become more stringent, and corporations spend billions to comply, the environmental movement must agitate for more complex, costly standards to keep the formula rolling.

And the formula is indeed profitable. The threat of headlines/public opinion/lawsuit drives the "charitable giving" considerations of many top corporations. According to Capital Research Center, a non-partisan think tank, for every dollar given to center-right, free enterprise advocacy groups, $4.41 was given to center-left advocacy groups – including the environmentalists. Clearly, the corporate blackmail formula works.

Equally important, the political strategies employed by liberal environmentalists have a baldly partisan aim – ending the Bush presidency. The idea is to demonize energy and industry, while portraying the Bush administration as willing accomplices. To that end, not one major environmental group has endorsed, or will endorse, even the most moderate of Bush environmental proposals – and there are plenty.

Perhaps the most vicious "safety/environmental" propaganda to date was unveiled when liberal-loving elitist Arianna Huffington funded, and Norman Lear produced, an absurd and insulting advertising campaign claiming that everyone who drives a sport utility vehicle is contributing to terrorism. Are the hard hats and soccer moms who rely on SUVs and pickup trucks for their daily work and to haul children to school *really* contributing to terrorism? During heavy snows, hospitals and local governments often call for SUV volunteers to transport medical personnel and patients. Are they contributing to terrorism? What bull.

The research I've extensively reviewed indicates SUVs are safe vehicles. The fatality rate (occupant fatalities per 10,000 registered vehicles) in front, side and rear impacts was 0.62 for SUVs during 1991-1998; for cars the fatality rates were at least twice as high in those types of crashes. And, according to the National Highway Transportation Administration, SUV rollover crashes represent only 3 percent of all collisions.

Since the late 1980s, Air Improvement Resource Inc. reports vehicle fuel efficiency has increased by about 1 percent. True, consumer demand for bigger, safer vehicles has offset this efficiency improvement, so the average fuel economy has remained flat since 2002. Yet, even so, fuel efficiency for cars has increased 133 percent in past decades and truck efficiency improved by about 75 percent. Its research also indicates that if no SUVs were sold during the next 10 years, U.S. oil consumption would only fall by 2.2 percent, worldwide CO_2 emissions would be reduced by less than 2/10ths of one percent and foreign oil important would rise from 55.5 to 56.7 percent.

Huffington, Lear & Co. don't want consumers to know that progress on SUV and light truck emissions reduction is impressive. General Motors' Trailblazer, Bravada and Envoy, for example, have lower tailpipe emissions than those of passenger cars on the road in 2003.

The Huffington/Lear ads, as well as the anti-SUV smears parroted by media reporters too lazy or prejudiced to get the other side of the story, are hypocritical; on abortion, liberals demand "choice" but with regard to transportation they seek to deny choice to consumers with particular needs.

Sadly, it's practically impossible to find the golden kernel of worthy endeavor in the shrill panoply that surrounds today's environmental movement. As the boy who cried "wolf" discovered, the long-term cost for declaring a daily crisis is that we may ignore a legitimate problem when one arises. If the radical environmentalist Dark Side succeeds in its current game, there won't be anyone around with means enough to answer the call if it comes.

⟳ Unchained Truth ⟳
Facts, Talking Points To Remember & Use

✳ The environmental movement pushes an agenda that is based on emotional scare tactics rather than solid science.

✳ The U.S. Environmental Protection Agency is a regulatory body, not a scientific body. As a huge government bureaucracy, it is slow to react to changes in scientific technology that will reduce the negative impact of industry on our environment. The new EPA Director, Christie Todd Whitman, is in the process of reforming the agency – with the promise of better science and better distribution of scientific evidence for the public.

✳ The Kyoto Protocol was a watershed for the environmental movement; its failure to pass the U.S. Senate due to its single-minded economic punishment of the Western industrialized nations is an optimistic sign that America will question the "truth" as given by the environmentalists.

★ We must question the political agenda of the environmental movement, because its basis in science is non-existent. Promoting polluters like communist China, India, and Mexico at the expense of the western democracies, who sustain the world economy and develop the "smart" technologies for energy use, flies in the face of common sense.

★ Aligned with social agenda-driven radicals in the Green Party here in the U.S. and abroad, the environmental movement is a politically savvy extension of the worldwide socialist movement.

★ There is no measurable evidence that fossil fuel use by humankind has made a measurable impact on the earth's cyclical weather patterns.

★ By threat of never-ending, high-profile and costly litigation and public relations wars, the environmental movement has successfully seized the funding necessary to continue its long-term campaign to damage American industry.

★ Sport utility vehicles are safe and vital to consumers and the U.S. economy — and the Dark Side's relentless campaign against them is insulting and hypocritical.

CHAPTER EIGHT

THE MARKS OF A DECADENT CULTURE

THE LIBERAL LINE

A new "diverse" America is preferable to the old America and its out-dated "God and Country tradition." The Eurocentric culture breeds racism, male domination and corporate exploitation. The rich get rich-er and the poor get poorer. "If it feels good, do it" is the freedom that ought to be encouraged, as long as we don't hurt anybody. There are no moral absolutes. The rules apply to those who "hurt" our society with their outdated thoughts and rigorous adherence to a moral code — and don't apply to those who "help" our society with modern thoughts and situational ethics.

UNCHAINING THE TRUTH

Reflect on this scene on a sidewalk outside a large Atlanta mall this past Christmas season:

A gang of male teens strutting by are checking out an attractive young female shopper. One audibly exclaims, "Yo! Look at that hot ho." Another has a boom box listening to some rap song rhapsodizing about a "brotha" pumping a .45 slug into somebody's head.

What a commentary on where the Dark Side has brought us culturally!

As the late U.S. Sen. Sam Ervin, D-N.C., used to proclaim in speeches, "Everything that was nailed down is done comin' loose!"

The folksy orator would have been particularly upset if he had lived to witness that mall scene and reflected on how badly America's cultural fabric has frayed since the Woodstock rock/drugfest..

Everything from the emergence of crude public behavior and crud as "art" to the undermining of America's traditional mores is there for all to see and for the pundits to debate. Just a decade ago the daytime TV soap operas – an interesting national barometer – wouldn't have been touting as "trendy" everything ranging from homosexual love to mocking the existence of a Supreme Being.

Incredibly, at the televised 2003 American Music Awards, a large portion of host Ozzie Osborne's family babblings had to be deleted because they were obscene. One principled actress, Patricia Heaton, even abandoned her part in the show and walked out in disgust. (Would that more would follow her example.)

Also – and get this! – in 2003, a degenerate Atlanta, Ga., group actually sponsored a "World's Famous Players Ball" saluting pimps, and the attendees were replete with men wearing furs and rhinestones the size of lemons. (A black clergy group and others picketed in protest, supporting the local U.S. attorney who initiated a crackdown on pimps who prostitute women and children.)

Historian Arnold Toynbee once noted, "Of the 22 civilizations that have appeared in history, 19 of them collapsed when they reached the moral state America is in now."

In light of that warning, even some liberals openly worried – but only after the impeached Bill Clinton left office – that his presidency, yes, was tainted because he admitted to lying and obstructing justice. So the "if it feels good, do it" philosophy apparently *does* have limits.

But what are the rules? That's the problem. Trendy liberalism will never present a coherent "rulebook" as to how it all works and what the limits are – thus giving free rein to its Dark Side.

Many liberals mock those who worry that the traditional family is under attack. But anyone with eyes and ears knows that most certainly is the case.

Parents, especially, feel their child-raising responsibilities are much harder than a generation ago. In fact, according to an October 2002 survey by Public Agenda partially funded by State Farm Insurance, parents worry most about whether their children will have good character and values—and they see America's popular culture as their adversary. Nearly half, 47 percent, said they were most concerned about shielding their children from negative social influences – and that included everything from illegal drugs to anti-social peer groups like those crude teens at the mall.

The large majority of American parents strive to model healthy heterosexual love and marriage to their children. And, of course, nothing facilitates this better than a parent or other family member keeping the lines of communication open, listening and displaying tough love with adolescents. Teachers and coaches form another line of support, especially with rebellious teens. Yet young people also get plenty of negative blather from the media, some peers and even some teachers.

Jesse Dirkhising was a straight seventh-grader who was brutally sexually assaulted and later murdered by two homosexual adults in a small Arkansas town in September of 1999. It was reported in some Arkansas media and, a month later, *The Washington Times* did a front-page story about the atrocity. But a media search at the end of November of that year yielded only a half-dozen news stories about it outside of Jesse's home state.

Contrast this media treatment with the coverage of the straights who murdered homosexual Matthew Shepard the year before. The left-wing *Washington Post* alone printed more than 80 stories on Shepard in the 12 months after the killing. The Associated Press put it on its national wire, so it was picked up by hundreds of other print, radio and TV outlets.

Such lopsided coverage highlights something many informed Americans have known in their bones for years: Liberals and open gays dominate many a newsroom in the mainstream print, radio and TV world. They don't want the general public to learn of the horrible things that some homosexuals advocate and do to straight children. They don't want their readers or viewers to know about, to take another example, the North American Man-Boy Love Association (NAMBLA) and its sick program of "inter-generational sex," which is nothing more than promoting the seduction of young boys.

If adult gays want to be tolerated (as opposed to being accepted), they should knock off the political lobbying and promotional propaganda which offends the large majority of their neighbors and co-workers. Their lifestyle, after all, is condemned by the world's major religions.

Yes, homosexuals should be free from verbal harassment or physical attack. Yes, everyone should be treated equally under the law. But homosexuals are doing themselves no favors when they flaunt their lifestyle and push for special preferences.

And why must the homosexual lifestyle be encouraged among high school students? Why must boards of education be forced to acquiesce in the "gay" lobby's insistence that *Heather Has two Mommies* or *Daddy's Roomate* has to be available in the school library?

Someone ultimately imposes their values on society. Why can't it be those who believe in the "God, family and country" values that made this country great? The choice is between moral absolutes based on historical and cultural norms, and situational, subjective ethical standards that shift like the tides of the ocean as culture "changes."

Most of today's liberals don't like it, but if they have studied history they must acknowledge that George Washington initiated civil religion for the new United States from his White House bully pulpit. Abraham Lincoln repeatedly invoked the term "One Nation Under God" long before the Congress voted to include the words "under God" in the Pledge of Allegiance to the flag.

After objectively examining the founding documents of this nation (including the Mayflower Compact), the U.S. Supreme Court found in the early 1900s that "we are a nation founded on certain religious principles." The first President Bush openly talked of trying to ascertain God's will before going to war against Iraq in 1991. Even Clinton paid the obligatory homage to "God and country" in some important speeches to the nation (especially after the Republicans took control of Congress during his tenure).

This civil faith, which honors God and country, is the root of public virtue in our nation today – and one would have to be blind not to see the cultural war that rages around us to decide whether or not our civil faith, i.e., the nation's Judeo-Christian historical tradition, will survive or become as extinct as the Dodo bird.

Take a look at just one ongoing battle in this cultural war. A federal judge in 1986 issued an amazing ruling regarding the Georgia city of Milledgeville's official seal. It contained the words "Christianity" and "Liberty" on a flag held by a woman sitting on an eagle—and, of course, the usual suspects went berserk. U.S. District Court Judge Wilbur Owens ruled the city could retain the word "Christianity" in its seal, but then turned around and said it couldn't be displayed where it would be widely viewed by the public!

Someone should have told that judge the best examples involving a historical recognition of America's civil religion are the Declaration of Independence, which holds that men are endowed by their Creator with certain unalienable rights; the oath of office taken by secular public officials, which concludes with the prayerful appeal, "So help me God"; and the national motto "In God We Trust," which appears on coins.

Catholic University law professor Robert Destro rightly called the 2-to-1 U.S. Ninth Circuit Court of Appeals ruling against use of the words "under God" in the Pledge of Allegiance "political correctness run amok." It was also left-wing grandstanding of the worst kind. Destro warns that if the appeals court verdict is ever ultimately upheld, it would make it illegal for the government to make any reference to religion, no matter how slight or obscure. That, of course, leads to a dangerous path because no one, especially America's children, would learn anything about the Christian religion or other religions.

For the Dark Side, though, that California appellate decision isn't radical enough. According to MSNBC *Hardball* host Chris Matthews, U.S. Sen. Hillary Clinton, D-N.Y., actually said she'd like to rewrite the Pledge of Allegiance to read, "I pledge allegiance to the America that can be."

What exactly does she mean?

Doesn't that mocking declaration give aid and comfort to those who now deride this country and its traditional institutions? Doesn't it mean that, to Hillary Clinton and her camp followers, America *as it is now* doesn't deserve our allegiance? She was actually caught in a unguarded moment of truth-telling!

William Bennett, former President Reagan's education secretary, probably gives the best rejoinder to those who would debunk our civil faith and replace it with some ethos of the pagan Left:

"The virtues of self-discipline, love of learning and respect for family are by no means limited to the Judeo-Christian tradition, or to any religious tradition. My point is that, in America, our civic virtues are inseparable from our common values. But it is the Judeo-Christian tradition that has given birth to our free political institutions and it is the Judeo-Christian moral tradition that has shaped our national ideals… It has content and power. All profit from it, although none is forced to assent to it. And, as the founders predicted, the constitutional order depends on it."

In contrast, the virus of political correctness becomes ever more corrosive. A civil society hinges on mutual respect between individuals and tolerance of different points of view. To the politically correct lobby, though, society is simply a battleground. It's a good versus evil conflict: white versus black; female versus male, gay versus straight, Anglo versus Hispanic, etc.

The oldest trick in the book, used expertly by liberal

politicians, activists and pundits, is the *ad hominem* attacks that, in effect, psychoanalyzes the opponent. For example, an opponent of race quotas is a "racist;" opponents of gay "rights" are "homophobes;" pro-lifers are "extremists;" a woman who doesn't work while raising children is a "victimized" throwback to the 1950s era. The list is endless.

Victimhood, of course, is the force that drives political correctness. The Dark Side has virtually canonized suffering, while attacking opponents for not being "compassionate" enough regarding whatever social program is being discussed. (By the way, one of the best counterjabs at the Left's celebration of victimhood occurred when then-presidential candidate George W. Bush's repeatedly invoked the words "compassionate conservatism" as one of his themes. It reassured wobbly independent voters who might be swayed by victimhood propaganda, while reassuring the conservative GOP base that the candidate was still "one of their own").

Consider a great cultural clash, brewing since 2002, that has ramifications far beyond the hallowed green fairways of the Augusta National Golf Club, home of the famed Masters golf tournament. According to feminist harpie Martha Burk, head of the National Council of Women's Organizations, the "victims" are women who aren't National members. The enemies are the members of one of the world's most exclusive private clubs who have chosen to retain an all-male (and, I might add, "all-wealthy") membership. That is the club's legal right, just as it is proper for the Boy Scouts of America to set its private membership rules.

And, just as it is the right of all-female Wellesley College (Hillary Clinton's *alma mater*) to bar males. And imagine if the Ladies Professional Golf Association was forced to allow men to play in its tournaments!

Several Augusta National members told me in early 2002 there was much talk among themselves about allowing the admittance of women into the club – but then Burk grabbed media attention (and found a way for her organization to shamelessly rally donors) with her letter attacking the Augusta club and its tournament. The outraged club chairman, W.W. "Hootie" Johnson, naturally felt he had to hold his ground at that point.

By the way, read some of Burk's writings. She is as anti-male as they come. In a piece for the Nov./Dec. 1997 issue of *Ms.*, the Augusta National nemesis presented her solution to the abortion debate: mandatory sterilization of men. She wrote that a man who had "unprotected sexual intercourse once a week" could "theoretically father 1,820 children. Add his increased years of fertility, and his potential for physical domination over women, and we can readily see that the problem of unwanted pregnancy is largely one of uncontrolled sperm."

"So," Burke continued, "how do we control men's fertility? Mandatory contraception beginning at puberty, with the rule relaxed only for procreation under the right circumstances (he can afford it and has a willing partner) and for the right reasons (determined by a panel of experts, and with the permission of his designated female partner)."

Burk said that "controlling men's fertility would not

be a hard restriction to enforce. The fertility authorities could use a combination of punishments for men who failed to get the implants and for doctors who removed them without proper authorization. The men could be required to adopt one orphan per infraction and rear her or him until adulthood. The doctors could lose their licenses or, in extreme cases, go to prison."

"Fertility authorities"? A "male one-orphan" rule? Martha Burk is loony!

Speaking of abortion, this burning issue will continue to separate Americans when it comes to politics and policy in the years to come. The U.S. Supreme Court's 1973 *Roe* decision legalizing abortion rightly rankles those Americans who feel the court majority legislated new law rather than interpreting state laws. Yet the current question on abortion is this: Will the vast middle of the populace start shifting to the pro-life cause?

Politicians who continue to throw the spotlight on the horrific practice of partial-birth abortion, which former Sen. Daniel Moynihan, D-N.Y., correctly describes as infanticide, are forcing people to think about, or rethink, their position.

Then there's the decision by the Supreme Court of South Carolina, the second one in a decade, upholding the conviction of a woman for causing the death of her unborn child. The court affirmed the conviction because of an already illegal circumstance: she was a cocaine addict. As a *National Review* editorial succinctly put it: "It may be criminal to kill a fetus by smoking crack, but one has a constitutional right to do so by using, say, a pair of forceps ... For 200-proof pro-choicers, a pregnant woman who smokes crack is no more culpable than any other crack user; for pro-lifers, killing a fetus in a doctor's office is no more acceptable than killing it with drugs." Such paradoxes ought to concern any thinking American.

Capital punishment is also vexing, and its opponents continue to highlight their cause. So let's cut quickly to the heart of this public policy issue. The main purpose of a sentence for a crime is to punish – not to attempt rehabilitation of a wayward soul, nor to "deter" other criminal from committing evil acts. Sentences are a way for society to exact a measure of retribution for actions that violate the norms of civilized society.

Therefore, the death penalty is the ultimate punishment equal to the ultimate crimes of aggravated, premeditated murder. While I say "equal to the ultimate crime," I dare say that victims' families would say in large measure that the death penalty is the *least* we can do.

Consider the moving testimony of a victim of the infamous Carr brothers, cited in the second chapter. A woman known as H.G., who survived a bullet in the head, described the killers as "soulless monsters" for whom a death sentence "will be much kinder than the sentence (they) imposed on me, my friends and all our families."

She concluded: "Every day there is a memory or a scar that reminds me of that night. While Reginald and Jonathan get to sleep peacefully in jail, I wake up in sweats from my nightmares. And every morning I carefully blow dry my hair to cover up the spot that can no longer grow hair. I look at my knees and see the scars from the carpet burns that I got from the rape and in the back of my mind I wonder, will it happen again?"

All this highlights a basic distinction between one philosophy – civic order and rule of law in a free society – and another more permissive philosophy that holds responsible society itself for the acts of "downtrodden" criminals. Ask H.G. – and the millions of other crime victims in our nation – how they view justice and cultural permissiveness!

∽ UNCHAINED TRUTH ∽
FACTS, TALKING POINTS TO REMEMBER & USE

★ The "coarsening of American culture" is, in fact, a direct threat to our existence as a free society. Where norms are subjective, right and wrong are situational, and hostile (and illegal) behavior is accepted as "society's fault," the rule of law fades into insignificance.

★ The Dark Side's rejection of absolute morals and norms has fostered the "us-against-them," group "rights" mentality that now polarizes American culture and government along racial, economic, and religious lines.

★ Noting America's moral, legal and ethical decay, historian Arnold Toynbee said, "Of the 22 civilizations that have appeared in history, 19 of them collapsed when they reached the moral state America is in now." As the only world super-power – and one based on the presumption of the dignity and liberty of the individual – America must reclaim its civic faith.

★ As individuals, Americans must reject the culture of permissiveness just as we reject the "group" mentality – both of which foster a violent rejection of the rule of law. Freedom is God-given, as memorialized by our Founding Fathers. But it is also contingent upon acting in the best interests of both the individual and society as a whole. When "society" becomes nothing more than various groups of angry people who live in proximity, people tend to act against the best interests of the whole. Mistrust breeds both apathy and violence.

★ America's civic faith promotes justice and embraces and protects the power and value of the individual to determine his or her destiny.

★ A congressional prohibition of partial birth abortion will help Americans think about, or re-think, supporting the pro-life cause. Although the Dark Side almost instinctively rides to the rescue of some perceived victim, when it comes to applying the death penalty for murder the victims and their families or loved ones are not to be seen or heard.

CHAPTER NINE

EDUCATION:
A CONTINUING BATTLE

THE LIBERAL LINE

Public schools are the most important service provided by government, because it's all about our children. Teachers are underpaid, school systems are under-funded, and federal and state education programs do not provide adequate resources to meet the needs of our children. Charter schools and vouchers rob our school systems of critical financial resources and, if allowed to occur, will harm public schools by robbing them of students and money. Education should be left to the experts who understand "modern" teaching techniques and know what's best for our children. In college, affirmative action preferences are needed to help minorities compete for admission.

Unchaining The Truth

"I was faced with coercion from students, parents and principals to give undeserving students grades. I was left to teach in difficult situations with little or no guidance. I was given the impossible task of preparing students, who could not write a complete sentence, for the real world. I witnessed careless use of classroom time by indifferent educators. I was also physically threatened by students and non-students because of my expectations."

That was the lament of Donna Arauz, a young high school teacher in Georgia's second largest city who told me that, by the time of her third year, "my desire to teach in the public school system was killed."

She quit, saying her desire was snuffed out "by the very people who need teachers the most – students and parents."

Her story is retold by others across the country – especially with "dumbed down" courses and assaults on teachers on the upswing in all too many public schools.

How did our nation get to this point?

First, some history.

The formation of public schools in America – at least in its current monopoly form – was basically an accident. As the late-19th century American population grew to proportions outstripping the ability of local, private and community-based schools to handle the influx, the public system of education developed as a response. Particularly in urban areas like New York City, where immigrants packed small geographic areas, it was expedient to develop a centralized system for maintaining some semblance of "equal" schooling.

Today, "education" funding represents more than half of most state budgets, and a significant portion of federal spending. Yet, recent studies indicate that, despite the fact that American public schools rank last in quality among the world's industrialized nations, public school funding – federal, state and local – costs more than twice what it did 20 years ago, nearly half a trillion dollars.

That's roughly $14,000 for every man, woman and child in the U.S.!

Education expert Susan Lacetti Myers notes that, between 1965 and 2000, the federal government poured over $100 billion into Title I schools with our poorest kids. In 2000, she found, $208 million of that money flowed to Title I schools in my home state of Georgia. Yet it didn't do a darn thing to help!

During 1999, 55 percent of third graders and 73 percent of second graders in city of Atlanta schools couldn't read on grade level. And, Myers notes, those kind of results are monitored nationwide.

(This sorry record in all 50 states is why President George W. Bush originally proposed in his "No Child Left Behind" bill that Title I schools that don't show progress must give the money to a parent in the form of a voucher so the child can attend a performing school.)

The late president of the American Federation of Teachers union, of all people, warned as far back as 1989 that "American education as it exits today will not be tolerated by the American people, by our business community, by our policy leaders for more than another few years."

In his speech to a national conference of teachers and school administrators, Al Shanker found that the mark of failure is *not* among the high percentage of illiterate "students" and dropouts, but rather at the low achievements of the so-called "successful" students – those who stay in school, graduate, and enroll in college. He raised simple questions: how many 17- and 18-year olds are able to read articles in our top newspapers, write an essay, or solve a two-step mathematical problem?

His answer: only 3 to 6 percent.

How many can write a simple one- or two-paragraph letter, perhaps for a job application? Only 20 percent of public high school graduates. When compared with foreign countries, he said that 90 to 95 percent of our high school graduates would not be accepted to any foreign university because of our relatively low entrance standards at many public universities in the U.S.

Shanker declared: "we have a Soviet system of education in this country." By that he meant the system treats all students the same, whether they are succeeding or failing. Just as the Soviet Union did everything in its power to confound and avoid "competition" to its oligarchy from free enterprise and democracy so, too, does the public education establishment fight good ideas like charter schools and school choice.

Shanker also noted that a primary distinction between foreign schools and American public schools is our emphasis on bureaucracy. "We spend half our money on bureaucracy, whereas the other schools in the world don't spend more than 20 percent."

According to *Reach for the Stars: A Proposal for Education Reform in Georgia,* published in 1991 by the Georgia Public Policy Foundation, American public schools have one teacher for every 25 students, and one administrator for every 6 students. Little has changed since that time.

The tired mantra of the National Education Association union is that higher teacher's salaries, smaller class sizes, and expanded facilities will improve education performance. Wrong. According to Brookings Institution analysts, "there is little reason to think that they will have any significant impact on how much students learn."

Sure, there are public school success stories involving dedicated teachers and students, many of them. But just as many, if not more, teachers like Donna Arauz, either burn out or are shunted aside in the haste of politicians and bureaucrats, as well as by well-intentioned but frustrated conservative and mainstream parents, who demand better results and more accountability.

And of our children, liberals and conservatives alike advocate for "the best." So, in that spirit, consider the following points as you prepare to take on the education establishment (starting in your very own community).

1. *Parents who care about their children want good schools.* This may seem like a basic point, but it merits consideration. Inner-city African-American parents, in staggering numbers, support school choice in the form of vouchers. Why? Because parents who care – of any color or background – share

a sense of responsibility for their children's future. Milwaukee welfare mother-turned-political activist Polly Williams galvanized the school choice movement when, in the 1980s, she organized the first successful school voucher program in America. Ms. Williams – politically, a Democrat – simply couldn't accept the fact that her children were locked into a failing public school system. She didn't have the money to move to a better suburban school district, and couldn't afford private schools for her children. Yet Polly Williams exemplifies for all American parents the simple fact that *we want what's best for our kids, and we can change the system to make it work for them.* So The Dark Side is finally facing a stiff challenge – because our allies are every parent who cares.

2. *Let's define our terms.* The terms "public school" and "public education" are effectively defined by the NEA and its allies as the buildings and bureaucracy that support the "education system." As parents who care, we should challenge this definition. Public education and schools are about children and their education – wherever, however that happens. Public schools are *kids*, purely and simply. Public education is taxpayer money spent to educate. The rest, including facilities, buildings, programs, administrators, and the bureaucrats who rule them, are the current, ineffective means for supplying our kids with education.

3. *Teachers are professionals, not old-style union dues payers.* The NEA is the single most powerful individual trade union in America. Its members comprise the entirety of the education establishment, from bureaucrats and administrators, to teachers and principals, to the Parent-Teacher Association

they've co-opted to approve their big-government agenda. Don't think so? Then how is it that the NEA can compel its members to pay dues, which are used to support the election campaigns of lapdog politicians who rubber-stamp the NEA's anti-choice, anti-reform program?

And how is it that the NEA, through many of its state chapters, can negotiate collective bargaining agreements for its members while threatening general strikes and walk-outs? Teachers in those states deserve better than to be pawns in a union's chess game, and our kids certainly deserve better.

Educators ought to be able to self-police and self-govern just like professionals do in the practice of law, medicine, accounting, and architecture, to name a few. Good teachers, above all, want the bad apples in their field removed far more quickly. Yes, teachers should be able to have an appeal process if they are to be removed – but state teacher tenure laws shouldn't be so tight that it is difficult if not impossible to eliminate the bad apples.

4. *School choice in the form of vouchers is not a threat to the public schools; it's a challenge because it's competition.* In every other aspect of American socio-economic life, we embrace and promote competition as a healthy way to encourage responsible prosperity – except in public education. Milwaukee's program, like its Cleveland counterpart successfully defended before the U.S. Supreme Court by my friend attorney Ken Starr, is straightforward: the local government gives a voucher to a parent who can choose to use it at any school for the sole purpose of educating a child.

Some conservatives raise a red flag at this point, worried that vouchers may mean government regulations on any private school accepting a voucher. These worries are not without merit; the federal government has a long history of "strings attached" when it comes to doling out public dollars. So let me issue a challenge in the form of a brief reflection about my home state.

The Official Code of Georgia contains Title XX, called "Education." Its 825-plus pages represent the sum of the collective laws regulating and controlling the state's schools. Of those pages, *only three* relate to private schools. To my mind, I would not support a voucher program that added one jot or tittle to those three pages – the government has yet to convince me that its 822-plus pages governing Georgia schools has made them satisfactory, let alone successful.

Let's also put to rest the biggest myth about vouchers – that they "take away" money from the public schools. It's infuriating to hear this lie espoused like fact on news shows and in newspapers. Let's get our facts straight: every school district in America has a per-pupil expenditure of public dollars, ranging from $6,000 to $15,000 per year, per student. Current voucher programs provide between $2,500 and $5,000 per year, per student. A single child who leaves the public school system takes away less money in the form of a voucher than he or she would have cost to support in the public school. One less kid, more money left over for the others remaining.

A second lie trouped out like clockwork is that "only the best will choose to leave with a voucher, leaving behind the worst students for the public schools." As a parent and as a conservative, part of me wants to say "so what?" So what that competition means public schools will either have to shape up or shut down. That's the point. But here's the real message: "good" and "bad" students alike benefit from better schools.

New York City's late John Cardinal O'Connor once issued a startling challenge to the city's political and education establishment. Confident that the city's parochial schools, among the most numerous and successful in the nation, could handle the onslaught, O'Connor told officials to send the bottom 10 percent of students from the worst-performing schools in the city, and he would guarantee successful education. Of course, city elders declined his proposal, but the point is made – whether parochial, Christian, non-sectarian, Jewish, Muslim, Montessori, or for-profit, the vast majority of America's private schools outperform the vast majority of our public schools.

5. *Charter schools, organized properly, are a good move for many communities.* There are now 37 states and the District of Columbia that have established community-run schools. Over 2,400 charter schools have opened nationwide just since 1992 that provide quality education utilizing public dollars. Teachers and principals – not to mention curriculum – are chosen by governing boards made up of parents, teachers, and those directly involved in the process.

But watch out! The state-level NEA chapters have taken heed and have urged "charter schools" to be approved by local school boards and governed by education bureaucrats and administrators. Insist on parent-majority control of a charter school's governing board as a prerequisite for state approval, or you'll be back in the same floundering public school boat you hope to escape.

6. *Reading, writing and arithmetic matter — more than ever, and more than social engineering experiments.* For nearly three decades, the NEA-driven education establishment in America has waged war against traditional curriculum, classroom competition, and basic ethical teaching, and for so-called "open classrooms," self-esteem psychology, "whole language" and politically correct curricula. Yet during the same three-decade time period, American public school student performance compared with that of students from all other industrialized nations has dropped. Harder math classes are definitely needed – Hollywood High School teacher Joan Gordon in Los Angeles, for example, says her failure rate in algebra is 60 to 82 percent because elementary and middle schools no longer teach good arithmetic courses. And, as far as the vaunted "self-esteem" training offered by many of today's public schools, how do you think our kids will feel about themselves when, once they are released from the feel-good cocoon of public school, they face the prospect of getting a job, earning a living wage, and dealing with the reality of our global situation?

7. *The key to change is public demand – so make your voice heard.* There is perhaps no area of government in which an active, vocal citizen can make such a direct impact than in the area of education. Local school board meetings are long and tedious, but board members are elected – remember

that. Take the time to attend some local board of education meetings. Also check the text of students' textbooks for historical misinformation, omission and political correctness. Insist that your board have a citizens' curricula advisory committee – and then get on it. And, while you're getting educated and involved at the local level, insist that your state legislators and federal elected officials stand for "back to the basics" education. If they don't, vote them out.

The window of opportunity for most parents is the few years in which their children attend public school. Most parents tend to lose interest in the need for sweeping reform once their children graduate. But, obviously, our nation's posture as a global leader depends utterly on how well educated and prepared our kids become as they reach college age.

Finally, let's reflect on illegal affirmative action – race and gender quotas or admission test "point" preferences – when high schools students or adults apply to colleges. Despite its benign name, most government-sponsored affirmative action programs are nothing more than institutionalized racism.

There's a dirty secret the Dark Side doesn't want you to know—not one government race quota program for public contracting has survived constitutional court scrutiny since the U.S. Supreme Court's 1989 Croson decision. The 2003 challenges to the University of Michigan law school, *Gratz v. Bollinger* and *Grutter v. Bollinger*, will go down as a landmark Supreme Court case with regard to universities. The main issue in this and other college admissions challenges, just as in public contracting cases, is whether there is an ongoing justification for using the legally protected, "suspect" class of race as a primary criteria for qualifications. So let's be clear when the Dark Side is confronted: Self-defined "diversity" by some university president for his or her campus should not be among the constitutional justifications for blatantly favoring members of one racial group over another.

Yet another secret the Dark Side relishes is that, during the 1990s, the number of non-U.S. citizens in graduate science and engineering programs grew by 18 percent. In the past 25 years, according to National Science Foundation figures, the share of doctorates in science and engineering earned by U.S. citizens dropped from 70 to 56 percent. The number of U.S. men obtaining these degrees each year declined sharply from about 12,000 in the mid-1970s to 9,700 in 1999. Nearly all growth of doctorates earned by U.S. citizens came from degrees earned by increasing numbers of white women and minority students.

The big question: Where are all those U.S. students who formerly pursued advanced degrees in physical sciences and engineering?

Harvey Shepard, a professor of physics at the University of New Hampshire, has an answer that makes the most sense:

"We live in a very divided land now – the increasingly visible wealthy and the working poor, with a dwindling middle class. This must generate a strange mix of feelings among the young: great anxiety and – at the same time – the fantasy of possibly being one who can strike it rich. In addition, most students leave college with a sizable debt. Combine all with the sense of entitlement bred in our culture by entertainment-dominated mass media, and you have a recipe for producing anxious, impatient, non-idealistic students, preoccupied with achieving economic security as soon as possible. This does not encourage the commitment to an often-lengthy graduate program involving the mastery of complex ideas and data."

I couldn't have said it better myself. In the 1970s many of my classmates at my alma mater, the University of Georgia, believed that if they worked hard and followed their curiosity they could pursue a graduate degree and then embark upon a career. The good New Hampshire professor is right. That sense of security and faith in the future has been lost. Somehow, conservatives have to figure out how to get it back.

ᏬᎧᎧ UNCHAINED TRUTH ᏬᎧᎧ
FACTS, TALKING POINTS TO REMEMBER & USE

✻ Schools are about teaching kids, not bricks and mortar. The only results that count are how well our kids are performing, and how well they are being prepared for life in a shrinking global community.

★ More money is usually not the answer. Despite ten-fold public education funding increases from federal, state and local governments over the past 20 years, overall academic performance by America's students ranks dead-last among industrialized nations.

★ The National Education Association has successfully defined America's education debate, while tying down the profession of teacher to nothing more than "dues-paying union workers." Teachers must be freed from the shackles placed on them by NEA-inspired bureaucrats, and should be self-governing like other professions such as lawyers, physicians, and accountants.

★ School choice – in the form of vouchers and charter schools – offers real competition to the monopoly held by government schools. Vouchers offer low-income families with children in the worst schools the opportunity to explore alternative schools, and charter schools are parent-governed community schools that know what's best for a child's education.

★ Vouchers do not "take badly needed money from public schools." In fact, most public schools spend twice as much per-pupil to "educate" a child as any voucher yet proposed. So, if a family gets a voucher and selects a private school, that's one less child in the public school system – with half the money otherwise dedicated to the child's education remaining in the public school system. (However, the NEA and its allies have learned that charter schools can be developed with governing boards consisting of a majority of bureaucrats and administrators. So, ensure they have governing boards with a majority of parents – otherwise, the charter school will mirror its purely government school counterparts.)

✷ Educational opportunity and competition are keys to social, personal and economic success. Ask Polly Williams, a former welfare mother from Milwaukee who, through persistent activism, made possible the first viable publicly-funded voucher program – a model for the nation's parents to encourage and demand.

✷ Check your public school textbooks for misinformation, omissions and political correctness. If found, complain to elected Board of Education members and speak out through the local media.

✷ Affirmative action preferences are nothing more than institutionalized racism. The Dark Side hates a colorblind America under the law – which is the goal conservative lawyers and legal foundations are fighting for.

✷ The number of U.S.-born science and engineering graduates are dropping, fueled by great economic anxiety and "the sense of entitlement" bred in our culture by entertainment-dominated mass media.

CHAPTER TEN

CARRYING THE DAY
WITH BIG MEDIA BIAS

THE LIBERAL LINE

Liberal journalists are constantly in danger of being muzzled by right-wing and corporate interests. Domination by conservatives of talk radio and the Internet, coupled with the emergence of the Fox News Channel, is drowning out the progressive reporters and opinion-makers. Many conservatives in the media peddle hate, and hate speech must be banned. Advocacy groups that utilize radio and TV during election campaigns, thus competing with the mainstream media, must be silenced.

UNCHAINING THE TRUTH

Many of us have seen it all before over the years. In the case of television, it could be the skeptical or mocking voice by the anchor or reporter. It is the omitted "other side of the story." It is the reporter's edited videotape that makes the business executive or the gun owner appear to be some crook or nut.

In the case of the print media, it is a supposedly objective "news story" that's slanted or even a smear against a conservative candidate, group or philosophy. Or, if the story is fairly objective, it's the headline that's biased.

It could also be the unflattering adjective placed in front of the conservative's name in the story as opposed to none in front of a liberal counterpart's name.

It can be subtle or blatant. It's left-wing media bias.

What is it all about?

It is about power. It is about who determines the norms by which we live and how we govern ourselves as a culture. And Lord knows, having been a newspaper editor and editorial writer myself, journalists love to tell people how to define and govern themselves.

Unfortunately, these days, the editors and staff for the daily morning and evening news shows, as well as the editors and editorial writers of all too many metropolitan newspaper dailies, are baby-boomer liberals who grew up on Woodstock permissiveness and anti-Vietnam war fervor. Their older mentors and protectors in the business are usually Roosevelt liberals or limousine liberal publishers like those who control the *New York Times, The Washington Post,* the *Los Angeles Times* and other big newspaper chains.

But there's hope. Most journalists enter the profession with an idealism bordering on zeal: *"I will be a watchdog for the people."*

This is a good thing. An open, free society like America, if it can still be called such, needs people like this. The good news is, most conservatives are reformers and share the same zeal for government accountability. Therein lies our common ground.

It is significant that ever since Vice President Spiro Agnew's 1969 speeches demanding accountability from "the tiny and closed fraternity of privileged men" who control the major newspapers and TV networks, critics of left-wing media domination are finally having an impact. Effective examples have been CBS-TV insider Bernard Goldberg's *Bias* and Ann Coulter's extensive documentation in *Slander.*

However, the purpose of this chapter is not to chronicle bias, but to examine the facts about the media and suggest how conservatives can break through and still get their message heard by the masses.

When I assumed the presidency of the Southeastern Legal Foundation, its communications director and my friend, Todd Young, handed me a book that is a must-read for every conservative activist. Aside from common-sense tips on everything ranging from making good first impressions to effective speech-making, *You Are the Message* by now-Fox News Channel president Roger Ailes contains valuable insights on how television, in particular, has changed all the traditional rules of media relations.

One of Ailes' best gems to remember is that, when someone on our side gets into a press situation, it is a natural adversarial relationship. "The reporter is a professional. Don't get into the ring if you are a rank amateur."

One might be surprised to find that many reporters outside of the big cities, especially those in their 20s and early 30s, tend to be basically apolitical or perhaps even centrist in their politics. They want to hear what all sides are saying on a particular issue or in a political campaign.

Thank goodness for these professionals.

Up until the late 1960s, reporters at most papers strove to be objective, with opinions essentially kept on the editorial pages. Then came the Watergate scandal and a trend of "advocacy journalism" in the journalism schools –the idea that a news story has to be "interpreted" so the unwashed masses get the big picture. It wasn't too long before reporters who did these interpretive stories and features got the promotions and salary raises over the traditional objective writers.

The pendulum may be swinging back more to the middle, though, in the journalism schools. At least there are now two schools of thought – with the left- wing *New York Times* still the Dark Side's prime promoter of slanted "interpretive" reporting.

But the bottom line is all journalists say they adhere to some standard of ethics (even ultraliberal *New York Times* editor Howell Raines). What we now face as conservatives is the obligation to remind journalists, especially editors, that there must be a standard of "fairness" to which they adhere, that such standard should be followed in covering XYZ issue, and that we are available to comment in print or camera.

Most reporters and commentators are plagued by deadlines and don't have the time or staff for effective research. Liberals have been effectively spoon-feeding these journalists their party-line and disinformation for years. Why? Because most conservatives, naturally suspicious of perceived media bias, refuse to deal with "the media." I have witnessed more conservatives than I can count, including elected officials, activists, and heads of national organizations, simply throw away phone messages from reporters. To a person, their response when I ask why is, "it's just gonna be a slanted story anyway, no point to responding."

Wrong. When a reporter calls, you answer. If you don't, you can guarantee that the eventual news story will not reflect your side. If you do respond, you have a fighting chance at being heard and covered.

Conservatives who "tithe" their money, whether in large or small amounts, have also helped unchain the truth through foundations. Think tanks like the Heritage Foundation, as well as legal and public policy centers like Southeastern Legal Foundation, ensure that effective repositories and distributors of information provide timely data that lazy or overworked journalists can't easily obtain. Bear that in mind when you consider supporting a conservative organization. Verify that it provides such information to the media. It's critical to the success of our war against the Dark Side.

TV personality Bill O'Reilly once said, "The media

keep you company, and they can entertain, inform and inspire you. That's good. They can also shape your opinions, behavior, tastes and desires. That's not so good. And they can be used by powerful people to seduce and persuade you and often lie to you. That's dishonest, sometimes downright evil and always there in your face."

His "no-spin" assessment led me to formulate two key rules for any non-liberal dealing with the media:

ONE: Be honest and unafraid with journalists.

TWO: Keep it concise; don't say too much.

When talking with a journalist, always start by establishing if your remarks are on or off the record. And get clear verbal consent. Roger Ailes also gives a warning:

"The main thing to keep in mind is that reporters are under absolutely no obligation to print what you say, but they can if they choose to, and you are under absolutely no obligation to tell them something that is damaging to you or your business."

After all, this could be a left-wing reporter on a witch-hunt against your business, your politics or your friends.

Instead of babbling general "inside information" to a reporter, keep your talking points concise. Then repeat the points, without giving new information, to help end the interview. Reporters may or may not like your candidate or viewpoint, but if you can feed them selected tidbits of interest about your candidate, or the opposition, it provides the ammunition a reporter needs to look to an editor like he or she got the "inside scoop."

I once read several comments in the Atlanta daily newspaper from friends who seemed all-too-eager to get their names in print. Georgia had elected, to the surprise of all the pundits, its first Republican governor since Reconstruction. Because the defeat of the incumbent was unexpected, most major Georgia corporations and political donors had contributed huge sums to the Democrat.

My well-intentioned conservative friends, still flying high from the heady victory, prattled on with the reporter about how corporations and lobbyists would "rush in with money to 'get right' with the new governor."

Not only did they *not* do themselves any favors with the new governor, who ran on an open-government, reform-minded platform, they were overly anxious to convey information better left for idle chit-chat around the water cooler – not for the front page of the daily paper.

The lesson here: Find out what the story is about before answering specific questions (reporters love to get specific without sharing the overall direction of a story), and ask yourself how you'd feel if you read your comments in the newspaper. If it doesn't pass the straight-face test, don't say it.

I've experienced the thrill and terror of appearing on many "talking head" programs on Fox News Channel, CNN, and CNBC, commenting on controversial issues. One of the best suggestions made to me before my first appearance some years ago was to watch myself on tape afterward. In the pressure cooker that is TV, it's difficult, if not impossible, to clearly judge yourself. But the tape tells all, from furtive eye movements to indirect answers to stammered points made amid the noise of multiple voices speaking at once. Preparation is key; know your messages ahead of time, and stick to them, regardless of what is thrown at you.

If there really is a blatant case of a TV reporter, radio talk show host, newspaper reporter or columnist who is out to "get" a candidate or a conservative organization, or out to distort or attack a conservative cause, aggressively fight back. Ask for fairness from the offending party first. If that fails then go to the supervising editor or even the owner. Write a letter to the editor of your local newspaper blasting the offender (these are usually published). If your letter is not run, get a group together to purchase an advertisement giving the same message as the censored letter.

Another option, especially if it is a conservative candidate or organization being attacked, is to strike back by use of direct mail or by Internet e-mailings. Attack your media opponents and link them to the actions of your political foes. (Or expose them for covering up for your enemies). Challenge advertisers to put pressure on the media outlet to be fair and demand that the offending journalist be reprimanded or fired.

You might even want to organize activists to picket the media outlet – which might be a great source of amusement to other journalists. Trust me, journalists are highly competitive and love to "gig" the other guy!

Sometimes reporters will just "miss" your side of a public policy debate, and you must respond immediately. The Clinton administration's vaunted "Masters of Disaster" media response team had a tough 24-hour rule for response, which made it incredibly effective at stymieing attacks from conservatives. (Many liberal newspaper opinion pages, stung by the exposure of their past bias, often will allow a conservative activist a guest column that can answer their editorial slant or news reporting. It can be an effective response tool.)

One last strategy is to approach a sympathetic pundit to promote your view. The pundit may make your crusade *his* or *her* crusade.

A case in point occurred when Pepsi-Cola announced it had hired the rapper Ludicris to do a commercial for the MTV awards. Pepsi executives thought that, since the thug rapper had sold millions of records to young people, those same mindless youngsters would emulate him when it came to drinking the soda.

Needless to say, not just conservatives but average Americans, offended by Ludicris' promotion of drug dealing and irresponsible sex and violence, were outraged. The aforementioned Bill O'Reilly, host of the Fox News Channel's "The O'Reilly Factor," became their voice and champion. After withering criticism by O'Reilly on his top-rated show, Pepsi dumped Ludicris and pulled the ad.

'Twas a famous victory in 2002. And it has been repeated. Whistleblowers, especially, shouldn't hesitate to contact sympathetic journalists in both the electronic and print media in order to expose some outrage by the Dark Side.

Some TV networks and daily newspapers scratch their collective heads trying to understand why viewership

and readership are down. Based on my experience as a journalist, these are the left-leaning news organizations. On the
other side, centrist-based news outlets, conservative talk
radio, and Internet news and information agencies like The
Drudge Report, WorldNet Daily, CNSNews.com and others, are flourishing.

Why? Because middle America has made it clear
that, once presented with an alternative to the stuffy, obnoxious elitism of the old guard media, it will seize upon it and
embrace it.

That's a very promising development for the future of
constitutional freedom in America.

ꝏ UNCHAINED TRUTH ꝏ
FACTS, TALKING POINTS TO REMEMBER & USE

✮ Is there a big-media liberal bias? Yes. Can conservatives
be heard by that same media? Yes. It takes patience, per-
sistence, and a willingness on the part of conservatives to
engage in consistent dialogue with reporters.

☆ Think through your positions before you speak. But speak out, nevertheless. You will not convince or convert reporters to the correctness of your position; their job is to provoke response to questions and elicit information, not debate with you. Your audience is America.

☆ The perception of a huge gulf separating conservatives from "the media" is simply wrong. Recognize that most journalists perceive themselves to be watchdogs for the people. Realize that most conservatives have the same goal – reform, fairness, and accountability from government. On that basis, guide your conservative comments to the media.

☆ There is no longer a single giant media establishment in America. Today, there are more than 100 conservative or center-right Internet news outlets, more than 600 nationally syndicated and local conservative radio talk show hosts, at least 200 center-right daily newspapers and a growing awareness among TV news programmers that the Fox News Channel "fair and balanced" approach is working. So, conservatives should be happy warriors for the cause. We can be heard, and we can influence the decision-makers!

☆ In most instances, Americans who happen to be conservative want to speak out only when provoked to respond to stories, issues and candidates. It's the liberals who tend to pontificate; as such, they tend to be more regularly seen and heard. So, if you want to write an op-ed article for your newspaper, or a letter to the editor, or speak out on behalf of your community or church group, take a deep breath; you can still convey your passion on an issue by relying on facts. Pure emotionalism will yield no coverage.

★ Get to know key reporters, at least professionally. Find out who reports on what subjects at your daily newspaper – most have email, and most return them. One or two phone calls, as well as a visit to various web sites, will give you a wealth of information on how to send a press release or news tip to a TV or radio station. Again, be clear, concise, and have your points thought out before you launch into your issue. But don't be a pest.

★ Whether you are an Internet hound or not, research various organizations that espouse your core conservative beliefs. In America, there are literally hundreds of solid groups who employ thousands of conservative thinkers, lawyers, writers and advocates who sacrifice big salaries in the private sector in order to defend the conservative agenda. These groups are the "tip of the spear," achieve results in the courts of law and public opinion, and generally do an outstanding job conveying our shared messages through the media. Get to know them, support them, and seek their counsel in preparing your own best defense.

CHAPTER ELEVEN

WHERE DO WE GO FROM HERE?

My astute friend, the late Lee Atwater, former chairman of the Republican National Committee, always had his pulse on public opinion. One of his last observations – one that has stayed with me – was that Americans "don't think they're getting straight talk from politicians. They don't think they're getting straight talk from the press. They don't think they're getting straight talk anywhere, really, in their lives. Bull permeates everything."

That analysis is just as apt today.

That's why, in the past 10 chapters, I began by reciting the main cliches of the Dark Side and then countered them with facts, talking points and action steps to help readers cut through "the bull."

Yet, having performed that task, a natural question arises: What are the arguments not extensively covered in previous chapters that favor replacing the corrosive liberal order with a new America that stresses traditional values, more open debate on public policy and common-sense, non-"politically correct" approaches to governance at the local, state and national levels?

Before discussing how to build this new America, I'm assuming that during the next 10 years our national leaders—prodded by massive citizen pressure – severely curb the massive tide of illegal immigration that threatens to permanently balkanize America and forever change our culture. I'm also hoping that mindless, out-of-control Third World refugee resettlement policies – which even includes placing people barely out of the Stone Age on the welfare rolls in major U.S. cities – will have been ended or severely curtailed.

I'm also assuming that a large majority of those illegally here will either have been somewhat assimilated into the majority culture, or deported. That would preserve the word United in "The United States of America."

Having made those important suppositions, I believe conservatives would be on solid footing to pursue three important missions that would vastly improve our country and its quality of life:

- ✪ Build – or, more accurately, rebuild – a culture of character.
- ✪ Honor true heroes – and educate future generations about them.
- ✪ Work to ensure the rule of law while curbing judicial activism.

✫✫✫✫✫

Our American culture is becoming far too decadent, as pointed out in the eighth chapter. It is stunning to contemplate that an R&B singer out on bail for 21 counts of statutory rape and child pornography could actually top the music charts, as R. Kelly did in March 2003. This pervert, just like convicted felon and movie producer Roman Polanski, is arrogantly unrepentant while being fawned over by the liberal Dark Side in Hollywood and segments of the media.

Who would have thought, just a few years ago, that such pedophiles would be above the law, or that young people – egged on by a dominant amoral cultural elite – would support their "entertainment" by buying their CDs or paying to see their movies?

Since the victims of these creeps are under-age females, where are the critical voices of self-described feminists who claim to support any sister in distress?

Whether they range from musicians to star athletes, right-thinking Americans must militantly resist Hollywood/media glorification of criminals and perverts. The tools to utilize in doing so are listed in the tenth chapter.

Matthew Spalding, director of the B. Kenneth Simon Center for American Studies at the Heritage Foundation, flatly states that "the revival of a culture of character is assuredly the greatest task we face."

We must restore the argument of the Founding Fathers, he underscores, that it takes both the workings of limited government and the proper dispositions and habits of the people to form good government and good character.

The Woodstock mindset of the late 1960s was revealed again, during the Clinton impeachment, when a chorus of the then-president's liberal defenders parroted there should be some sort of wall separating personal conduct and public character. Of course, those same liberals threw in cliches about "tolerating" their Bill Clintons and "moving on" while continuing to damn any public figure to the right of Ted Kennedy for "politically-incorrect" opinions and flogging corporate America as the real epitome of selfishness and immorality.

A 2002 Heritage Foundation meeting in Philadelphia was properly devoted to the topic of character, and panelists examined two forces – politics and pop culture – that help erode character. Then panelists proceeded to emphasize a corrective I heartily commend to readers. To cultivate virtue among the general populace, they agreed, there has to be more moral accountability.

This is in line with the great thinker Aristotle, who taught there could be no liberty without people of virtue. And while it is no guarantee, a good dose of revived religious faith among the masses is crucial to accountability.

In the faith I was brought up in – Christianity – Peter instructs Christians in their responsibilities to human governments. We are subject to kings and presidents, we are to pay taxes and we are to actually pray for leaders of our government (even if they might be horrible!). Government is supposed to protect people and their property, punish law-breakers and promote the general welfare of society. That's what the Judeo-Christian tradition teaches and, by the way, this is right in sync with the preamble to the U.S. Constitution.

Yet, the Dark Side constantly attacks what is right and true. A college professor once mockingly asked if I believed in "absolute truths." I said yes. I thought most others did, too. Yet, in recent years, national polls have consistently found a majority of respondents saying they didn't believe in any absolute truths.

That's one reason why this country, and especially its governing bodies, needs more accountability – a clear sense of right and wrong.

Why are politicians rated so low in the polls? Why do people get tired of, as Lee Atwater said, the "bull" emanating from them?

For one thing, it's just human nature that people can't abide other people they perceive as self-serving. So every politician or judge ought to remember that he or she is accountable. They also should learn from their mistakes (or the errors of others) – especially that pride and hubris can quickly precipitate a fall from power.

Members of the executive, legislative and judicial branches, especially, had better take heed when it comes to abusing privileges. (Furthermore, they shouldn't have any privileges forbidden to their constituents!)

Finally, while noting that a revival of religious faith will help rebuild a better America, that faith is never more undermined when it is used to excuse moral weakness. That, in my view, is the major lapse of the clergy who slavishly follow the Gospel of St. Trendy – and why liberal churches are losing members and more traditional houses of worship are experiencing an increase.

☆☆☆☆☆

Many Americans today are fascinated with the lives of celebrities, which is fine. But all too many confuse being a celebrity with greatness. The comings and goings of leading actors and actresses are far better known by the general public than the activities of, say, religious leaders. Recall when the U.S. mainstream media launched into an orgy of coverage over the death of Britain's "fairy-tale" Princess Diana, yet, that same year, virtually ignored the passing of the great healer and teacher Mother Teresa.

That's why – in analyzing "where do we go from here", conservative activists must push to ensure that our young people and future unborn generations rediscover and honor genuine heroes. We've got to get more parents and, when we can pressure them, taxpayer-subsidized educational institutions teaching about real heroes who stood for the right principles.

C. Bradley Thompson. chairman of the history and political science department of Ashland University in Ohio, attended the 2003 meeting of the American Historical Association, the nation's most influential organization of historians. Reflect on his observations:

"Of the roughly 200 panels, there was virtually nothing on subjects such as the American Revolution, the Civil War or America's involvement in the two world wars. Instead, there were dozens of papers on subjects ranging from the banal to the bizarre and perverse.

"Participants were subjected to presentations on topics such as 'Meditations on a Coffee Pot: Visual Culture and Spanish America, 1520-1820,' 'The Joys of Cooking: Ideologies of Housework in Early Modern England' or 'Body, Body, Burning Bright: Cremation in Victorian America.' But without question, the dominant theme of the conference was sex. Historians at America's best universities are obsessed with it."

Thompson's lament is a call to arms. Let's venerate, first and foremost, the founders of this country who gave us such cherished documents of freedom like the Declaration of Independence and the U.S. Constitution.

Can you believe that, during the 2003 General Assembly in supposedly "conservative" Georgia, a Democrat state representative named Bob Holmes actually told colleagues he would have no part of approving legislation encouraging students to study and recite parts of the Declaration – one of the greatest documents of Western civilization? It was a "myth," said Holmes, the chairman of the state House Education Committee. "It was insulting to blacks."

Another lawmaker reminded him that slavery was worldwide at the time, and even whites were held in slavery or as indentured servants. Yet Holmes insisted the document is a myth, even though it launched the most prosperous and free government on the planet.

There are others like Bob Holmes, of course, in all 50 states, and this mindless attitude starkly illustrates what we are up against.

It is also offensive that the third Monday in February has come to be known in popular terms as "President's Day." February 22 is the birthday of George Washington, a true hero instrumental in bringing about the Constitutional Convention and who more than any other founder made possible the birth of our republic. The absurdly-named "President's Day" – generally commemorated by stores hawking mattress discounts – ought to officially revert back to a celebration of this statesman. Congress could pass a law directing all federal entities to refer to the holiday as "Washington's Birthday," or the president could perform this service by a simple executive order.

Restoration of a George Washington holiday could be accomplished. Just look at the model of how a few conservative leaders mounted an effective PR campaign, and Congress quickly went along, to rename Washington's National airport after former President Ronald Reagan. Our first president should still be "first in the hearts of his countrymen." After all, his transfer of power in 1797 to his elected successor started the democratic tradition of a peaceful transition of leadership that remains unbroken to this day.

The Dark Side lauds the anti-hero – those who defile our culture, or sneer at patriotism and uncomfortable truths. New York City's Brooklyn Borough President Marty Markowitz is a case in point. In 2002 he took down the portrait of Washington that had been hanging in the Borough hall office. Washington was just "an old white man," he said. "There's not one picture of a person of color, not one kid, not one Latin Borough Hall should reflect the richness of our diversity."

But his action revealed the true meaning of liberal "diversity": Extinction of our heritage and its replacement by others.

The unheroic in politics are those guided merely by the latest polls – and who are saved or influenced only by the integrity of others. Our heroes should be those who fight for truth and champion good over evil. The hero also protects the innocent and helpless.

Like Washington, who are some other real heroes?

My favorite poet, the late E. Merrill Root, once eloquently addressed that question:

"(H)e is a Nathan Hale, giving up a brilliant career for his country, and dying in the noose of a spy ... he is a Pickett and his men in gray, charging hopeless into the Union guns in Gettysburg ... he is Keats writing his great Odes under the smog of stupid critics, with death in his lungs ... he is Henry David Thoreau, dying too early, and saying quietly to a friend who asked him if he had made his peace with God, 'Why, you see, I never quarreled with Him" ... she is Emily Dickinson, dying unpublished and unknown, but writing to the end the great poetry 'too intrinsic for renown' ..."

A hero never falters under attack – just like a Gen. George Patton Jr, who won brilliant military victories for his country and, in spite of his many jealous and hateful critics, never compromised his integrity nor renounced his God or his hatred of godless communism.

Then there are countless religious martyrs. One introduced to me by my parents stands out – the Rev. Richard Wurmbrand, who helped spread "underground" Christianity in Romania when it was controlled by a Communist dictatorship. I once heard him testify to such heroes:

"The following scene happened more times than I can remember: A brother was preaching to the other prisoners when the guard suddenly burst in, surprising him halfway through a phrase. They hauled him down the corridor to the 'beating room.' After what seemed like an endless beating, they brought him back and threw him – bloody and beaten onto the prison floor. Slowly, he picked his battered body up, painfully straightened his clothing and said, 'Now, brethren, where did I leave off when I was interrupted?"

Jesus is the ultimate hero, and our Western calendar is marked before and after His death. Liberal clergy like to paint Him as merely "meek and mild." While he performed wondrous miracles, healed the sick and was an apostle of love, Jesus also taught the world the meaning of righteous indignation by brandishing a whip, overturning the tables of the money-changers and chasing the defilers out of his

Father's temple. It was Jesus who said the corrupters of children ought to have a millstone hung around their necks so
they could be thrown into the sea.

The poet Root once taught that as a man or woman
finds the great meaning which he or she must serve, and as
he or she consecrate themselves to such service, there is no
talk about being a "hero."

Often they don't even realize they are being or acting heroic.

Remember the New York City firefighter who, after
the Sept. 11, 2001, attack, told a TV reporter: "When people run out of buildings, we run in. That's what we do."

That's a modern hero!

Todd Beamer, who rallied fellow passengers on
United Flight 93 to overpower and kill the hijackers of his
doomed plane on that same fateful day, is yet another.

It should be the duty of every patriotic American to
foster a culture of character and to teach children, grand-
children, nieces and nephews about this country's founding
documents and true heroes the world has known as opposed
to mere Hollywood celebrities.

☆☆☆☆☆

As to the third aspect of "what is to be done?" one has
to reflect that the rule of law must be firmly upheld while, at
the same time, vigorously curbing increasing judicial
activism. The American Revolution wasn't fought and won
to achieve self-government only to have that self-gover-

nance nullified by a few unelected activist judges paying homage to the Dark Side.

Whatever one's political philosophy, one ought to be concerned that courts have taken over legislative powers through:

1) a claim that a vague constitutional clause not only prevents a state, prison system or a school district from implementing some policy, often leading to an order implementing some other policy and;

2) the inability of Congress to meaningfully restrict judicial review.

Thomas Jefferson, in a Sept. 28, 1820, letter to one William Jarvis, says:

"You seem to consider the judges as the ultimate arbiters of all constitutional questions; a very dangerous doctrine indeed, and one which would place us under the despotism of an oligarchy. (The) Constitution has erected no such single tribunal, knowing that to whatever hands confided, with the corruptions of time and party, its members would become despots. It has more wisely made all the departments co-equal and co-sovereign within themselves."

Professor William A. Stanmeyer, who has taught constitutional law at Georgetown and other universities, effectively examines how another founder, Alexander Hamilton, wrestled with the problem of possible unconstitutional acts by the judiciary itself. (A case in point: The example in the fifth chapter of the Ninth Circuit Court of Appeals nullifying the Pledge of Allegiance to the flag.) Stanmeyer writes:

"The Court, Hamilton tells us, may nullify acts of Congress when the latter violates specific constitutional prohibitions – e.g, passes an *ex post facto* law or bill of attainder – or where it passes acts 'contrary to the manifest tenor of the Constitution.' *Manifest* must mean obvious, clear, undisputed. Again, Hamilton remarks that in ascertaining the meaning of the Constitution, as a fundamental law, the judges must ascertain the meaning of any particular act preceding from the legislature. 'If there should happen to be an irreconcilable variance between the two,' the Constitution is to be preferred. Irreconcilable suggests only those cases where no reasonable man could find a way to reconcile the statute and the Constitution; otherwise, an ordinary variance, one that can be harmonized by skillful interpretation of either statute or Constitution, would not warrant striking down a congressional act. And, finally, Hamilton urges that the judges 'should be bound down by *strict* rules and precedents, which serve to define and point out their duty in every particular case that comes before them.' It should be apparent that if the judges follow strict rules and precedents, they will not come up with bizarre interpretations of vague phrases or reverse meanings in their own prior decisions."

Stanmeyer concludes that since the U.S. Supreme Court and the other federal courts do not even show the self-restraint that their own philosophical defender, Hamilton, would require, it is time to find a way to return to the original purposes of the Founding Fathers, and create an *institutional* check on the runaway power of courts.

How many times have we as Americans seen one

unbridled federal judge wander off into a political reformist mode, regardless of any heed to the Constitution or case law precedent?

Often, rather than spend huge amounts of money to fight this lower federal court judge, public bodies ranging from state legislatures to housing authorities have thrown in the towel and surrendered. I have always thought, since my early days of print journalism editorializing against judicial tyranny, that Congress should clearly define the grounds for impeachment of a federal judge to include such decisions as ordering expenditures from any taxpayer-supported body without that body specifically approving the money.

The 1973 U.S. Supreme Court decision *Roe v. Wade* was a classic radical grasp of power from the 50 state legislatures on the issue of abortion. *Roe's* author, Justice Harry Blackmun, even attempted to demonstrate that traditional American law didn't seek to protect the unborn – a galling and highly questionable proposition. Even some law professors who are abortion advocates concede that *Roe* wasn't well reasoned.

What better example of a radical ruling to understand that America can't stand for the U.S. Senate to confirm any more activist judges to the Supreme Court and other federal courts?

That's why the bitter 2003 confirmation fight over President George W. Bush's federal appeals court nomination of Miguel Estrada was so important. If leftist Democrats – although a minority in the Senate – ultimately succeed in filibustering to death strict constitutional constructionist nominees that a Republican president sends, the Dark Side will have won big-time.

The Republican Party, despite it flaws, remains the best vehicle for promoting the overall conservative agenda – and part of that agenda is to place into positions of power better judges than the ones Jimmy Carter and Bill Clinton left this country. Republican senators – and those Senate Democrats like Sen. Zell Miller, D-Ga., who believe in strict judicial adherence to the U.S. Constitution – need to be supported in the public arena during what will be a protracted years-long struggle for the heart and soul of America's judiciary.

I'm an optimist. It is possible to attain the three goals I've outlined because, not so long ago, a rising tide of "noble" liberalism seemed vibrant, confident and on the winning side of history. That's not the perception anymore. More and more liberals are embarrassed to even be identified as such. They often have to cloak their policies under phony, innocent-sounding labels.

Today, in the sage words of columnist Jeffrey Hart, "liberalism is making the great refusal. It seems to see life, in Robert Frost's phrase, as a diminished thing. It is defensive and shrunken and it has opted out of the American tradition." The profound negativism of today's liberal defines, Hart notes, the conservative opportunity.

So it does.

The conservative, when realizing what is to be done and how to persuade others to help, ought to fight for future goals with an optimistic eye and a fearless heart.